Helen Bogus
November
1991 — Rochester, N.Y.

The Three Faces of Love

The Three Faces
of Love

BY

PAUL A. HAUCK

THE WESTMINSTER PRESS
PHILADELPHIA

Book Design by Dorothy Alden Smith

First edition

Published by The Westminster Press ®
Philadelphia, Pennsylvania

PRINTED IN THE UNITED STATES OF AMERICA
2 3 4 5 6 7 8 9

Library of Congress Cataloging in Publication Data

Hauck, Paul A.
  The three faces of love.

  Bibliography: p.
  1. Love. 2. Marriage. I. Title.
BF575.L8H35 1984   158′.2   83–10468
ISBN 0–664–24486–6 (pbk.)

JACQUELINE HAUCK
and
ROBERT FIELDING

I dedicate this book to you
for all the love you gave mom and pop

Contents

To the Reader

Love has three faces: appreciation, forgiveness, and firmness. Love is anything but being endlessly nice and unswervingly giving. The latter idea, that love is what we get when we sacrifice ourselves enough, is the source of an enormous amount of neurotic and physical suffering.

Few concerns are more misunderstood than is love. To achieve cooperation, respect, and love from the significant people in your life it is essential that you learn to overcome four emotional disturbances: fear, anger, guilt, and other-pity. The contributions from Rational-Emotive Therapy (RET) can teach you the basics for this control.

In addition, you'll need to learn about the reciprocity theory of love, the business theory of marriage, and the three rules for getting cooperation, respect, or love. How and when to apply these theories and principles is the subject of this volume.

After reading this book you will be informed on the subject of love as few people currently are. Thus educated, you will be better prepared to understand and deal with those many problems which come into everyone's life concerning how to love and be loved.

1
The Problem of Love

It is one of the most desired conditions in the world. People seek it all of their lives but seldom get enough of it. It is a commodity for which people have an insatiable appetite. The more they get, the more they want. It creates feelings of the most intense delight such that, with its first encounter, people remember it forever. However, it is also one of the most painful conditions. People kill themselves and others over it. It is on the minds of the masses to such an extent that probably no other subject has been expressed in so much song, poetry, and prose.

Without it the infant dies. Without it the adult becomes emotionally misshapen. It is a powerful thing, but it is very unstable. Because of it we sometimes exhibit the very best within us, and sometimes it causes us to exhibit the very worst within us. In short, it is one of the most misunderstood subjects in the world.

What is it? Love, of course.

Throughout my years as a clinical psychologist in public and private practice I have come upon countless clients who had difficulties in their love lives and in their marriages. For many years I was at a loss to understand many of these problems because, frankly, I had no philosophical framework by which to guide myself. As my experience increased, however, I gained insights into the mysteries of

11

love and marriage and began theorizing and writing about them.

One of the insights I gained was that more people were disturbed over their love lives than over any other single problem. They might come to me exhibiting such emotions as depression, anger, anxiety, jealousy, or excessive passivity; and sometimes these emotions would be in connection with their careers, disciplining the children, or perhaps even financial matters. However, the single most frequent life situation that precipitated any of these emotions was clearly the troubled marriage or romance.

LOVE DISORDERS

The subject of love is probably one of the most misunderstood subjects in the whole world. Here are examples that illustrate how unaware of the problems of love some intelligent, educated, and professional people can be.

It has not been very long ago that I heard this piece of advice given over a television show. A doctor was advising a female patient whose marriage was in difficulty; and after listening very patiently, he leaned over and put his hand on the patient's hand, patted it a few times and said with a loving smile, "I think what your marriage needs, Mary, is to have another baby." I used to think this was only soap opera stuff until I ran into my own clients who told me how often they received this advice from their friends, clergymen, or doctors. To me this clearly signifies that these advisers have little or no appreciation for what makes a marriage tick. In truth, that advice might well have been sensible for only the most minute percentage of the married population. The vast majority of married couples do not need another child when their marriage is in difficulty. To burden a woman with another child when she has serious difficulties with the other children or with her husband is pure insanity. If a man wants to leave a marriage because of the difficulty he is having with his wife and his children, or because of the financial burdens he must wrestle with daily, the suggestion that he take on another child will only increase his frustrations and financial strain.

The fact that such ludicrous pieces of advice are given in all seriousness shows clearly that most of us haven't the foggiest notion what causes marital discord or how to solve it.

Industry is also peculiarly ignorant on this subject. Even large companies having excellent health benefits for their employees often will not include marriage counseling as one of those benefits for which the company will pay. They will pay if one of their employees is depressed over the loss of a pet, or if a man cannot sleep because someone banged into his car, or because a worker is worried about the health of someone in his or her family. But they will not pay to help a husband and a wife who are not getting along, regardless of what symptoms they are exhibiting.

What could be more important to a company than to have husband and wife emotionally happy with each other? And what could be more destructive to a company than to have two people not getting along? Should a company pay for such services? In my opinion, absolutely! It doesn't matter what the particular cause may be; the fact that the consequences can be devastating is the only consideration we need bother with. And marriage counseling is the method best suited to help two people get along with each other within a marriage.

Just how unaware we are of the difficulties inherent in handling love and marriage sensibly is illustrated by the enormous difficulty we have when trying to decide on two of the most important questions that will ever confront us in a lifetime. The first is, "At what age should I marry?" and the second is, "Whom should I marry?" Neither one of these questions has been answered by research in any

definitive way. At the present time these matters are han-
dled mostly by the heart, not by the head. Although we
can get some sensible direction from listening to our feelings, we are apt to find the way only if we are fairly mature
people to begin with. When disturbed people listen to
their hearts, they wind up infinitely more disturbed. It is
not of much help, therefore, to suggest to immature and
troubled people that they make critical decisions in their
lives based on their own immature personalities and their
troubled feelings.

In spite of all the research that has gone on in the social sciences, little headway has been made in helping
people know when and with whom to spend the rest of
their lives. It has often been said that we can put a man
on the moon but we can't cure the common cold. It is
also true that we can put a man on the moon but we
can't tell our young daughters or sons when the best
time is for them to marry and with what kind of person
they would be happiest.

It seems to me that it is high time people became aware
of just where love is located with respect to the major
human motivations. Is love the greatest of our drives and
motives, or is it among the weakest? It turns out that love
is at about the midpoint between the most basic and the
highest motivations.

Abraham Maslow, a psychologist who formulated a theory of motivation, suggested that we are all driven by five
motives. The most basic motivations are the strongest, and
when they have been reasonably satisfied we develop interest in the next set of motivations—and so on up the
pyramid until we come to the fifth level of motivation. In
their rank order of importance they are as follows:

1. Physiological needs
2. Safety needs
3. Belongingness and love needs

4. Esteem needs
5. Self-actualization needs

We cannot, of course, dispute the fact that physiological needs are the most basic. When a person is hungry, cold, or thirsty, nothing else in the world matters except food, clothing, or water.

All of us feel better if, once the body has been fed and watered, we have someplace that will protect us from the elements and the danger around us. It is at that time that our external environment and our physical safety become almost as important to us as our internal environment. It is for this reason that we like to have homes, lock front doors, live in a predictable world, and know where our loved ones are and when they are coming home. Children uniformly thrive better in a family where there is some semblance of scheduling and order. The future is more dependable for them because they know what is going to happen.

Next come the needs for belonging and love. And why not? After all, the inside of the body is now well taken care of and the environment is reasonably controlled, so it is time for us to bring in another human being with whom we can associate intimately. People want to have affection from others, to have companionship, to ward off loneliness, and to be able to satisfy sexual appetites as well.

Note carefully, however, that this need for belonging and love ranks third in the list, not first as many people seem to think. Judging by everyday behavior, we would gain the impression that the only thing people are interested in is love, love, and more love. Actually this is the impression we get only because we have our physiological and our safety needs so satisfied that most of us don't give them a second thought. If suddenly our food supply were endangered or a tornado tore the house off its foundation, however, I can assure you we would not think about going to a dance tonight. We would be worried about whether or not we had a roof over our heads.

Needs for esteem gain importance next, after we feel we have been loved and are acceptable human beings to others. It is at this time that we want to strive for achievement, to demonstrate adequacy, to show the world that we are competent and that we can be independent and free. This is also the time in our lives when we want to have prestige, recognition, and attention for our efforts.

The last needs on the list are the needs for self-actualization. These are our desires to become all that we are capable of becoming. Self-actualization is the total and complete fulfillment of our inner destiny.

When we look at these five needs we can perhaps begin to appreciate a bit more the vital, but not preeminent, place that love has in the scheme of things. Needing love is a temporary phase in our growth which leads us on to yet higher motivations such as self-esteem and self-actualization needs. Let us, therefore, always consider the drive for love and acceptance as neither the strongest nor the weakest of motivations. It is a prerequisite for the higher motivations and can be reduced in importance once it has served its purpose of lifting us up to the fourth and fifth levels. Just as we do not concern ourselves with finding food in order to survive each day, so we do not look about us every day for proof of our worthwhileness (by being loved and approved of by people) once we have passed that stage.

The last point I wish to make—which may prove to you how truly unaware we are of love as a human condition— is that love has never become a designation in psychological diagnosis. I think it could be.

What name would you give to the condition of someone who is intelligent, well-adjusted, and handsome or beautiful, but who suddenly becomes depressed, tearful, and insanely jealous, and is perhaps ready to commit suicide?

All of us have either gone through such periods of temporary disturbance ourselves or know of people who have been through them. We all know someone who has been so madly in love that he was willing to lay down his life for the woman of his dreams—or someone who would give her life for the man who has fulfilled her fantasies! When a high school football star comes to therapy ready to die because his girl friend has broken up with him, are we dealing with a simple case of depression? Are we dealing with a transient adolescent disorder? Are we dealing with a long-standing and ineffective personality problem? I think not. We are dealing with a condition which I have called "the love disorder."

The love disorder is a very painful or exhilarating condition similar to manic-depressive psychosis. It has the same capability as a psychosis of making you feel as though you were flying on wings of song or sitting in a dungeon. This is a condition that afflicts both young and old. And it is sometimes the most deadly the first time it hits. In any event, it causes us to lose our reason, to forget every other important thing that our lives are concerned with: to forget food, drink, sleep, and work. If that isn't a neurotic reaction, what is?

It is not a laughing matter when you see a person actually suffering the intense agonies of an unfulfilled love desire. Such people suffer in unique ways, and they suffer intensely. It is not enough to teach them to stop blaming themselves so that their depressions end. What is required for lasting health is for them to fall *out* of love. Falling in or out of love is like going in and out of debt. The first step is easy, the second is anything but.

The psychological and psychiatric professions are not yet well acquainted with this diagnosis. I am not certain they would accept it if they were. I feel this is a mistake; and as we become more sophisticated in our knowledge of love as a human condition, we ought to recognize it for all its beauty and all its danger by giving it a diagnosis along with the other painful emotions.

CAUSES OF THE PROBLEM

There are essentially two broad reasons why we have trouble in our love lives: faulty thinking and faulty interpersonal strategies. By faulty thinking I am referring to the irrational beliefs we have been taught by our families, schools, and society. (A list of twelve such irrational ideas will be found in Chapter 4.) As long as we follow these false paths we are bound to run into problems.

We manage our lives better when we attack our problems on both fronts: when we challenge irrational thoughts and when we change self-defeating interpersonal behaviors. I shall spend considerable time in this book on both approaches. One without the other is not as helpful as both are together. That's why a knowledge of how to think and how to behave is so crucial.

To teach you the subject of healthy thinking I will rely on the contributions of the Rational-Emotive therapists. The material on interpersonal behavior strategies comes largely from my observations in my clinical practice over three decades.

The rational control of our emotions is essential if we wish to love and be loved. There are four emotions in particular that make the attainment of cooperation, respect, and love extremely difficult to achieve. They are fear, anger, guilt, and other-pity. I know of no theory of emotional disturbance as helpful in this regard as the ABC theory of emotions (which is explained in Chapter 4). I also know of no other course of instruction that helps teach the cause and control of those four emotions more efficiently than Rational-Emotive Therapy. Chapter 4, "The Other Cheek," describes the techniques you can use to control these problems.

In discussing why loving couples quarrel and eventually fall out of love, I do not intend to go down a long list of obvious reasons. Rather, I want to give you some insights from my many years of counseling people with marriage problems. Just what are those issues which create misunderstanding, distrust, and hostility between two people who started out with a beautiful dream and will end up having a nightmare?

If I were asked to identify the most common underlying failure that men and women have in a marriage that has become inefficient, self-defeating, and highly stressful, I would have to say it is *the failure to realize how important it is for a person to maintain a reasonable degree of satisfaction in his or her marriage.* Too many people have been taught throughout the years that the best way to get someone to love you is to give in to the other person endlessly, and that the more you give, the more love will be returned to you.

This statement needs to be qualified. If it means that you are having your own needs and desires satisfied at the same time that you are pleasing your partner, then well and good. However, if you are constantly sacrificing without reciprocity, the marriage will almost certainly be in serious trouble. It is my observation that being *very* passive, loving, and giving creates stress. One of the best remedies for this is to learn how to become assertive. In brief, I find that one of the best cures for a bad marriage is to teach one of the parties involved, and sometimes both of them, how to get *more* benefits from the marriage. I will explain in the next chapter why this is so vital in making the feelings of love grow and in making a marriage work. For the moment, simply keep this comment in the back of your mind as you read farther: *Most unhappiness in marriage occurs because one or both of the partners have sacrificed too much.* Being thoughtless about your own desires and needs is ultimately not only bad for you but bad for your children and partner.

A person who is obsessively concerned about another's welfare develops problems of possessiveness and jealousy. Instead of allowing the other person the freedom that goes a long way toward enhancing the feelings of love, the tendency is to smother and stifle those wonderful feelings in the other person. Too many adolescents have been told that the more we love someone, the more we will be loved. That sounds beautiful and mature and, if carried off properly, is in fact a workable ideal. Unfortunately it is an ideal that easily becomes perverted and turns into a series of one-sided interactions between a giver and a taker. Any relationship that becomes unbalanced, with one partner giving a great deal and the other receiving a great deal, will simply end up being a sick relationship. We must base our marriage conduct, not on total sacrifice for the other person, but on a reciprocal sacrifice schedule. This is a mature and healthy approach rather than a selfish one. And it should be free of guilt.

Regarding the balance between how much one person has to give as contrasted with what another person expects, the important consideration is not how much you are giving to your partner but, rather, how much you value what you are getting.

One of my male clients told me once that he had a very happy marriage because his wife gave him everything he expected. I was rather surprised at this remark because I had always thought of him as someone who had been denied a great deal. His wife appeared to a number of my associates as a rather indulged person. He maintained, however, that all he wanted from her was that she should stay home and take care of the children, keep a nice home, and be faithful to him. For these benefits he was willing to exchange practically anything she asked for. She controlled the family finances and could stay out late, buy clothes and jewelry, and even go on some vacations with her relatives or girl friends. He got what he wanted and was quite content.

Dr. Albert Ellis, the founder of Rational-Emotive Therapy, has suggested that there are essentially two kinds of incompatibility: neurotic and profound. Neurotic incompatibility is that which exists between two people who basically are well suited to each other but who, because of temporary emotional difficulties, are not getting along well. Clear up the emotional hang-ups and things go along smoothly. As a matter of fact, most of the people who come to marriage counseling are precisely of this type.

Profound incompatibility, on the other hand, stems from differences between the partners so great that a peaceful coexistence is almost unthinkable. For example, a very religious person is almost bound to be extremely unhappy living with an atheist. One of my female clients was very much in love with a man and wanted to marry him, but, because he was not a Christian, she simply could not entertain the thought of ever living with him. That was a profound incompatibility and I agreed with her decision completely.

Other forms of profound incompatibility have to do with such issues as whether disciplining the children should be firm or lax, whether money should be spent or saved, or whether sex should happen twice a day or twice a month. These incompatibilities are so very fundamental to the values each of us treasure that to have them in our own homes is more than a frustrating experience, it is a *profoundly* frustrating experience.

One of the major reasons for these differences in the way two people approach problems is their upbringing. Family backgrounds are much more important in determining how a person deals with issues and adopts philosophies than is generally appreciated. There are a great many persons who see me with difficulties in their marriages precisely because they did not take the cultural and social background of their partner into consideration when they married. One woman, for example, was surprised that her husband lacked ambition, spent hours in front of the television set, seldom helped around the house with the children or the dishes, and would routinely take off with his buddies on fishing or hunting trips. Yet when I explored his background, it turned out that his father was very much like this, and his mother always tolerated it. So my client had married a man who was raised in a home where the father went to work, returned home, rested up, and had his social life separate from his wife's. So why shouldn't this woman's husband be the way he was raised? Had she paid the slightest bit of attention to the home from which her husband came, she would have been able to predict fairly accurately what her own husband would be like.

One of the strongest pieces of advice I have for people who are engaged is to spend as much time with your future in-laws as you possibly can. Observe how they treat each other, what their political and religious views are, how they deal with money, and whether they quarrel or calmly talk things out. Be around them so much that you can catch them in their off-moments. And then make some rather hard-nosed decisions. What you see in that family is more than likely what you will be dealing with yourself. Do not make the naive assumption that your future husband or your future wife will be vastly different from what you are looking at in his or her family. People behave as they are raised. They can surely change, I agree. However, those changes are down the road quite a piece. In five or ten years your fiancé may outgrow picking his teeth with a fork. But you can rest assured that the philosophies, the temperament, and the life-style with which your lover was raised are going to be an integral part of the relationship you will have for a good many years.

This brings us to another poorly understood fact that

causes friction in otherwise healthy relationships. It is the tendency on the part of people to undergo normal and repeated changes throughout the years. The one whom you married when you were in your early twenties will not be the same person when you are thirty. When he is around twenty, a young man may be interested in riding motorcycles and getting drunk with the boys, and may want to play more than work. When he is about thirty years old he may give up motorcycles for economy cars, he may change his friends from the rowdy bunch to the more business-minded or intellectual kind, and he may simply settle down in other ways that would have been considered boring and unthinkable when he was a younger man.

Of course, the same applies to women. They may undergo changes from being passive and dependent on their husbands for decisions and for support. As they grow older they become less fearful, more independent, and more grown-up; and their husbands may not enjoy living with these changes.

I find that people change fairly regularly about every seven to ten years. I recognize that these are very imprecise figures. Whether changes come every five, seven, or ten years is not as important, however, as is the fact that you can depend upon people changing. And this is one of the reasons that divorce happens even after many years of marriage. It merely signifies that enough time has passed and enough changes and growth have taken place in one (or both) of the lovers that the things that made him or her happy at one time no longer do so. We are, after all, changeable human beings. And it should come as no surprise that we usually want different things as we go through life.

I maintain that a marvelous thing often happens to people when they reach the age of thirty or are somewhere between twenty-eight and thirty-two. It is in this age span

that many people for the first time are able to understand
what life is all about. They can look back over the previous
years and understand them in an entirely new way. They
can get insights into their own behaviors that were totally
inaccessible to them before. It is as though they have been
walking uphill through a dense forest and have finally
reached a clearing and are able to look back and see where
they have been. For many, that is what it's like to be thirty
years old.

The psychological and practical meaning of becoming
thirty is that this is often a stressful period for marriage.
The person who has just attained thirty may begin to
change in very healthy ways, and this can sometimes be
of great annoyance to the partner who may not like these
changes. Men, for example, will often become more assertive and goal-directed, and in general act more maturely.
Women frequently become less dependent (thus less cooperative), and in general become less fearful. To an insecure man this obviously presents serious problems. If he
has not profited greatly by attaining the age of thirty and
his wife has, then we have a pronounced imbalance in
terms of maturity. If she becomes very mature at this point
in her life and he does not, then she will think that she has
a child for a husband, instead of a man.

A further cause of friction between many partners is
that they do not realize that maintaining a marriage is
simply one of the most difficult of all normal human en-
deavors. Marriage requires enormous dedication, patience, and the acceptance of long-range responsibilities
that are often crushing in their intensity. A young woman
who had been married for only two years made the point
to me that marriage is stifling, demanding, inhibiting, and
often difficult. Yet she did not want a divorce; she was very
happily married. I feel that she had an entirely correct
understanding of her situation. Those starry-eyed, naive,
and romantically dazed youngsters who think that being

married is going to be a perpetual holiday are doomed to a rude awakening. When they are unable to pay bills, or one ignores the other unfairly, when he no longer has his freedoms because he has a family to support, or she finds herself confined at home because she has two babies who need constant attention, then for the first time they will begin to realize the true meaning of marriage and its heavy commitments.

I want to make it absolutely clear in this book that I think marriage is a wonderful and beautiful institution. It is one of the most rewarding of all human activities when successfully performed, and I urge most people to attempt it as a way of achieving long-range happiness. Thus I believe we had better spell out to young couples the entire reality concerning what marriage actually is all about. The drudgery and the pain, the frustrations and the hurts, along with all the blissful moments, need to be explained so that people are not surprised when it rains on their parade.

Another impediment to marital harmony comes from our lack of appreciation for the very subtle but profound differences between men and women. Leaving the obvious physical differences aside, one has to see a number of people in counseling and listen to what they have to say about one another in order to catch the prevailing complaints that come out in session after session. For example, it is positively fascinating, and a little bit strange, to note how frequently women from different backgrounds will come to counseling and make similar complaints. I have half jokingly told any number of my female clients that they must all have met out in the hallway prior to coming into my office and decided to give me the very same story. Yet the truth of the matter is that over the years I have learned to anticipate what most of the female clients—and most of the male clients—will say in complaining to me about their spouses. This consistency of viewpoint has con-

vinced me that there are certain innate differences between men and women, not just differences in the way we
bring up our little boys and girls.

Some examples: When a little boy becomes a man it is
simply not very difficult for him to separate love from sex.
He can have an argument with his wife one moment and
want to take her to bed the next. In short, he can think of
having sex with a woman and not care in particular about
her as an individual. Men frequently make complaints of
not getting enough sex from their wives and that they are
being too possessed by the women. Men often feel that
they demonstrate their love for women by working hard
for them, not getting drunk, coming home on time, and
being faithful to them. They do not see why it is at all
necessary to say "I love you." What are words compared
to actions?

Women, on the other hand, far more often talk about
wanting affection and love and do not mention sex at all.
It is not that they do not like sex, but love and affection
embrace sex. It is as though these qualities, love and sex,
are inseparable. Therefore, it is very difficult for them to
engage in sexual behavior without having a great deal of
fondness for their lover. To engage in sex casually is meaningless for them. It is debasing, and it makes them feel as
though they are being used "like a piece of meat."

Another common characteristic of women is that they
like to talk about how they feel, and they want to know
how their lovers feel. The communication of feelings is for
them an absolute requisite for sexual satisfaction. For a
woman not to know the person she is sleeping with
amounts to prostitution. If she cannot know what is going
on in the heart of her mate, she will not want him as a
mate. Deep feelings, therefore, and the communication of
these feelings, are more important than holding hands,
buying a new dress, or taking a trip. Unless he is someone
to whom she can bare her soul as well as her breast, she

often is simply not interested in him. That is a fact of feminine psychology that a great many men do not understand, do not appreciate, and often do not like. When we speak of the strong, silent type it is understood that we are speaking of men. Women usually are not strong, silent types. Although they certainly may be strong, they are often not silent. Women want to express themselves. They enjoy the release of feelings and the sharing of intimacies, and they want to know exactly where they stand with those with whom they interact. Men, on the other hand, do not need to know the inner recesses of the minds of their wives. And when they are troubled, they often don't even want to communicate their troubles to their mates, because they feel they should work things out by themselves. Women, however, often say that if they cannot talk about their problems, they'll "go crazy." It makes a difference to whom they spill their troubles. It must be someone whom they respect and who has a sensitive ear and a soft shoulder. A man often doesn't care for such things, and he finds much more comfort in being able to deal with a problem himself. It is not always a matter of his being self-conscious about talking over his problems with others, or trying to avoid being thought of as weak, though either may be true at times. The major reason he does not want to talk about all of his inner complaints is that it simply is not necessary for him to do so, since he can or should deal with them himself.

A further source of irritation between lovers stems from the impossibility of actually pleasing the partner enough to prevent a separation or divorce. Not all problems have nice solutions. Not all marriages can stay together, no matter how much one might dearly desire them to survive. And those who do not understand that some marriages are simply doomed to failure, even though they struggle vigorously against that eventuality, make themselves and their partners miserable.

For example, suppose a man after fifteen years of marriage decides that he is no longer going to fight the rat race and wants to give up a life of ambition and accomplishment. His wife, however, is still very much materialistically oriented. She wants a man who is going to give her a fine life-style and the wherewithal to enjoy clothes, cars, and lovely vacations.

These individuals may quarrel because of their divergent goals without realizing that arguing is pointless. Sometimes people simply take views on which they cannot compromise. She wants the good life, he wants the relaxed life. At this time in their lives they cannot have both together.

A phenomenon I call "catching up" further illustrates the inability in some instances for a married couple to resolve their difficulties. Catching up happens when a young man or woman marries too early and misses out on a lot of the fun that he or she might have had if the marriage had taken place years later. But since it did not, there comes a point in the lives of these people, perhaps at around thirty, sometimes at around forty, when the man or the woman wants to have freedom, to have other partners, or to get on a motorcycle and drive cross-country in a burst of adolescent excitement, simply because it is something that he or she never experienced.

If a man feels cheated because he married early and never had a fling, he must either learn to accept that fact and live with it gracefully or be willing to put his marriage in great danger.

What partners say to each other in the heat of a fight and under the influence of great anger has a great deal to do with the future course of their marriage. Some marriages that had every possibility of prospering and growing in harmony were destroyed because one partner impulsively and repeatedly declared while in the heat of anger: "Get out. I want a divorce. I can't stand you. I hate you. I never should have married you."

Such statements are not always devastating. However, if they are repeated over the months and years, you can be sure that the words begin to cut deeper every time they are said. One wants to be forgiving and tolerant of such scenes for a time, but, when they go on and on, one loses patience and begins to believe that perhaps the other partner does want a divorce.

My suggestion to all married couples is to keep your angry mouths shut. If you don't know how to control your anger, then learn how. Do not shoot your mouth off in the heat of a battle just because you want to hurt your partner. You will regret this practice because you will lose points every time it happens. The day will arrive when there is no longer any feeling between the two of you. Eventually your mate will say: "Okay, if you feel that way, I'll go. You'll get your divorce. You finally convinced me this was all a mistake."

There are two more causes of marriage problems that I have saved for discussion until the last. As long as both of these conditions exist, there will always be plenty of business for marriage counselors. The first has to do with the irrational notion that when people marry, they "belong" to each other. People get the idea that to marry someone is to have acquired a piece of property. When they say, "You're mine," they aren't always using poetic or romantic language. They are using legal language. They mean: "You are mine, you will do as I say, you cannot go where I don't allow, you cannot talk to anyone I disapprove of," and so on.

Those who never take this property idea seriously fare much better in a marriage. They know that a marriage is an agreement and that it may be a *temporary* agreement between two people who have accepted the understand-

ing that they have a contract only as long as the arrangement works to a reasonable degree for both of them. They
fully understand that when an arrangement is no longer
satisfying enough, either individual has a right to end the
relationship and that it is sensible to do so.

Unfortunately, those who are insecure, who feel inferior, and who are supersensitive about their own self-
worth, often do think of their husbands or wives as property. They don't agree that people have the right to end
the relationship. They believe that having a ring on the
finger is equivalent to having a ring through the nose. And
these are dangerous people. Often they are jealous, vicious, and angry to a psychotic degree. I met a man once
whose wife told him she was leaving. He invited her to
meet him, and she did. He then proceeded to murder her
by strangulation. I interviewed and tested this individual,
and much to my surprise I found that he was not psychotic
or mentally retarded. He was about as normal as most of
us are. However, he believed that she had no business
talking to him that way; that she could not break a promise
once she gave it; and that if he couldn't have her, no one
else could. She "deserved to die" for trying to leave him,
is the way he put it.

The last cause of friction in marriages that I want to
discuss is the need to be loved. People will simply sit and
look aghast at me, with mouths open, when I point out to
them that love is not necessary in life. It is as though I
have said something blasphemous. Along with flag,
mother, and apple pie, love itself has been enshrined as
an object of our sacred loyalties. He who does not regard
love as the highest spiritual goal is thought of as being an
animal. He who does not make love a second god is an
unfeeling robot. It is claimed that everyone must have
love, and that life is unbearable and horrible without it.
It is said that rejection is the greatest of insults and the

worst danger a human being can face, and that only in the love and approval of other people can we measure our own value. Such is the importance given to the whole concept.

Rational-Emotive therapists routinely find that an irrational idea largely accounts for this distorted view of love. The irrational idea goes as follows: Unless one is loved and approved of by significant people, one is not worthwhile.

The neurotic *need* for love, rather than the practical *desire* for love, has caused more pain in people who are supposed to love each other than any other single thing. We try too hard because we think we *have* to have love at all times. We sacrifice ourselves ridiculously, make doormats out of ourselves, become dictators, develop depressions, angers, and jealousies, and fill ourselves with fear, all for the noble purpose of being loved. Ladies and gentlemen, it is time that we looked at this subject more realistically!

Why do you have to be loved? I know the answer to that question in reference to children: they would die without someone caring for and loving them. But I am now talking to you as an adult. If you are well into your teen years and older, stop acting as though you have to have the love of your mother or family. What would happen to you, for example, if they all died? Would you go up in smoke? Would the earth swallow you up? Would you suddenly become a big glob of nothing? Since when does somebody else's loving you make you a worthwhile human being? Weren't you worthwhile before you were loved? Will you let other people pass judgment on you through their love or lack of it, and decide from that whether you are worthwhile or not? There has to be something wrong when you turn such an evaluation over to other people who have no expertise concerning you. Why should any other person be able to tell you whether or not you are acceptable?

Think these things over very carefully. Ask yourself again and again whether or not the love of other people is really *critical* in your life rather than very *desirable*. Isn't being without love inconvenient, regrettable, and sad? Of course it is. But is it also horrible, terrible, and tragic, and does it mean the end of the world? If you think so, prove it.

Do not be misled by this last point. I am in no way against the deep feelings people develop for each other. I think they are positively wonderful, and I urge people to work very hard toward developing intimate relationships with those they care for. Life is so much nicer when those we care for care for us. But I do take exception to the idea that one *has* to have love constantly from that one particular person. That does not make sense.

If you understand this point, you will forever be protected against the greatest fear people have: rejection. Rejection is tò most people like a dagger in the heart. It is a deathblow. It is a sentence to hell. It is the agony of all agonies. To be rejected by people we desire is to many of us the ultimate proof of how absolutely worthless we are. If we had worth (so we imagine), we would never have been rejected.

But rejection is painless, *unless you make it hurt.* If you insist that you have turned into dirt because your lover has rejected you, then you never had much of an ego to begin with. If you think that your life is over because your husband has taken an interest in someone else, then you never had much confidence in yourself. If you think that because your lover is not talking to you the end of the world has come, you obviously have very few coping resources. In other words, the reaction to rejection, if it is a severe one, is simply a reflection of your own inadequacy and inferiority. You have been taught to believe in the bogeyman. You have been taught to believe in ghosts, superstitions, witches, leprechauns, and Easter bunnies. That's how much sense it makes to say that you, a well-functioning and intelligent adult, need the love of another person. I want to remind you how often you have broken up with loved ones already. Yet when your other relationships dissolved, you were able to survive them time after time and were able to find other people to relate to. Despite these repeated experiences, you may still be repeating the same falsehoods to yourself: "It is horrible to be rejected. I am going to die. It proves I am worthless." And so on.

Enough of this! Let us grow up. Let us give ourselves credit for all the struggles we have gone through in life and consider rejection as just another frustration. Let us see ourselves as capable of recovery from these annoyances. Let us give ourselves credit for coping capacities that enable us to adjust to new societies, new countries, new jobs, new families, and the whole growth process itself. We are not children. We are adults. We are strong. We are capable. And we are desirable to many people in the world, even though perhaps not to our present partner. So be it. Life will go on and our lives along with it.

THE SOLUTION

The following chapters will describe "the three faces of love" by offering three separate rules you can follow to show love or receive love. Instruction is also given on how to control the four emotional disturbances that can weaken the operation of those rules. I first came across Rules No. 1 and No. 3 in the work of psychologists Charles and Clifford Madsen. Rule No. 2 comes from religious tradition.

The Madsens wanted to teach children that *(a)* when

they did nice things, nice things happened to them, and *(b)* when they did bad things, bad things happened to them. They pointed out that these two simple principles were often disregarded and children were taught to expect entirely different consequences. The consequences children actually expected were as follows: *(a)* when children did bad things, nice things sometimes happened to them; *(b)* when they did nice things, bad things were likely to happen; *(c)* no matter what a child did, bad things happened; and *(d)* no matter what a child did, nice things happened.

Let us return to the Madsens' first two principles, which seem to me to be very sensible but incomplete conceptualizations of what actually happens between two persons. I would like to add a middle step and thereby formulate three rules for achieving cooperation, respect, and love.

Rule No. 1: If people treat you nicely, treat them nicely.

Rule No. 2: If people treat you badly, continue to treat them nicely, turn the other cheek, go the extra mile, and love those who trespass against you, *for a reasonable period of time.*

Rule No. 3: If people treat you badly, *and the second principle does not work,* treat them badly with approximately equal intensity, and without anger.

The beauty of this conceptualization is that it is based on scientific understanding and is simplicity itself. I do not want to mislead you into thinking that it will therefore be easy. You will find that achieving cooperation, respect, and love with any of these three methods is going to be hard work indeed. But you will find at least that the world is not confusing, and that you can keep your sights on the goal through all kinds of subtle complexities. As long as you know where you are going and why, even if you have only a general conception of what you should be achieving, then any number of elements can enter into the picture and you will always know what your response to other people's behavior can be.

Before we can delve into that, however, it is extremely important that you have a clear picture of what love actually is, and how, and why, marriages work.

2

The Truth About Love and Marriage

THE RECIPROCITY THEORY OF LOVE

Love is that powerful feeling which one has for persons, animals, or things that have satisfied, are satisfying, or will satisfy one's deepest desires and needs. This may not sound like a very original statement, but I assure you that a closer examination of it will reveal a great many insights not easy to accept.

For example, the definition clearly indicates that it is not people that we love, it is rather what the people or animals or things do for us that we love. (In this book we will not refer to animals and things but will concentrate on persons.) If the person you love does not satisfy you in ways that are extremely important to you, it is my contention that you will simply fall out of love with him or her. If there are no satisfactions, benefits, or pleasures from that person, the love dies. The contrary is also true. The more someone satisfies your deep desires and needs, the more you will be tempted to love that individual. But bear in mind again, basically it is not the individual you love, it is *what the person does for you.* Once you understand and accept that simple fact, you will find it a great deal easier to create in others a feeling of love for you. You had better be a realist in this or you will not succeed. But once you accept reality and understand what is the true meaning of love, you will not fight your inclinations to give your partner what it takes for him or her to love you.

For example, if your partner wants you to have hygienic habits, then the more fastidious you are in your dress and in the care of your body, the more that person will love you. If it is also important for your partner to have much affection, then obviously the more you satisfy your partner's affectional needs by touching, holding hands, sitting side by side, and giving a warm embrace spontaneously, the more that person will love you.

And what about physical appearance, money, earning capacity, and life-style? Do we also love people because they are rich, they dance well, or they are honest? That depends upon the values of the person making the judgments. If certain qualities are important to you, then you will naturally fall in love with people who have those qualities. Other people may have all kinds of other wonderful characteristics, but they will simply not interest you because those are not important qualities in your particular case. This means that if financial security is important to you, or if a rich life-style is one of your dreams, then you will naturally fall in love with someone who has wealth.

You may protest that this is not a demonstration of love, but only a deep caring about money. In other words, you might claim that it is not the person you care about, it is the person's money. If this is what you are thinking, then you have failed to understand the point I made initially. One does not care for people unconditionally, one cares for what people do for us. If money is important to you, then it is not only the person you love, it is the money the person has, and the willingness on the part of that person to share it on your behalf. So money can become as legitimate a reason for loving someone as physical appearance, neatness, good sexual performance, or any other behavior that you happen to value.

But what if the financial security begins to diminish?

Could a recession wipe out feelings of love in a family? You bet it could. Feelings of love can go down just as fast as the money in the bank does. And that's the way it is with all of the desires you have. The more they are satisfied, the more you are in love. The less they are satisfied, the less you feel in love. If you want a husband who is strong, makes decisions, and will defend you against his family, and if you find that your partner does not meet these expectations, I can assure you that your feelings for him will diminish in direct proportion to the number of times he disappoints you. And if you want a wife who has a lovely figure and your partner begins to put on pound after pound, I can assure you too that your feelings of love will begin to fade as her pounds begin to increase.

I know that you must think that this is a rather immature, crass, and totally unacceptable conception of what marriage is. And I, of course, agree that it is anything but romantic in nature. However, it is realistic. This is the way people are, like it or not. We behave toward each other precisely in these ways, and I have had many years of clinical experience to prove it.

You may protest that people certainly aren't always loving others just because they are being treated kindly at the time. Surely there must be many instances when we love others and expect nothing in return. I disagree, but you must understand that I am talking about *intimate love,* not *fraternal love.* Intimate love has to do with one's partner, parents, children, relatives, or close friends. These are the people who affect us in our daily lives and for whom we are willing to make enormous sacrifices. When I am talking about my theory of love I am talking about the normal process of reciprocity that always takes place among *intimate people.*

Fraternal love, or love of humankind, is a very noble human sentiment also, but it does not require a similar expression of love in return. You may have been one of those generous persons who sent a CARE package over-seas to destitute families in a devastated country. You probably simply gave your check to the organization and hoped that it would bring good fortune to someone thousands of miles away. You did not care particularly who that person was, you did not expect an actual expression of thanks through the mail or phone or in any other way. You did a good deed and you were happy in your heart that you were able to have enough good fortune to share this with someone else. The reward was knowing you had reduced someone else's suffering. That is nonintimate love, the love one has for one's fellow human beings. It does not require reciprocity. In a sense it is, therefore, more noble than intimate love, which sooner or later does require payment for effort made. However, this is not totally accurate either. Fraternal love works as it does because we are only occasionally asked to make sacrifices for people we don't know. It doesn't matter, therefore, whether they pay us back or not. But if they were to need us on a continual or almost daily basis, I can assure you we would regard them, not as distant people whom we wanted to please, but as very important people in our lives from whom we wanted to have some payment in return. That is one of the essential differences between intimate love and fraternal love. The former involves constant contact with people who are dear to us, while the latter involves practically no contact. The former involves frequent sacrificing for one's loved ones, while the latter calls for a mild and infrequent sacrifice. Therefore, I stick to my point that when it comes to an intimate relationship in your life, you will give to the other person as often as you feel comfortable and as long as you feel that you are getting a reasonable amount of satisfaction in return.

But what about our parents who are now aged, retired, or senile and who can no longer pay us back for all the efforts and expense we are putting forth to care for them?

If you will recall my definition of love, I said that it was a feeling that we have for people who *did* (in the past), *do* (in the present), or *will* (in the future) satisfy our deepest desires and needs.

When we think back on all the wonderful efforts our parents made on our behalf but are not able to continue now because of old age, we can pay them back for the lifetime of sacrifice they made for us when we were younger. We still want to reciprocate and pay off our indebtedness to them because we love them so dearly for the many efforts they made for us earlier.

But what about our children? What can a child do for you that would make you love the child? Surely the amount of benefit a child receives from a parent is enormously greater than the benefits the parent receives from the child. If the reciprocity theory of love holds true, how do we explain the great love that a parent has for a child?

Our benefits come in several ways: Children please us enormously and satisfy our deepest desires and needs by: *(a)* proving that we can become parents, *(b)* perpetuating our own species, *(c)* carrying on the family name, and *(d)* often proving to be absolutely delightful, wonderful little creatures who bring great joy to our lives despite periodic disturbances.

IMPLICATIONS OF THE RECIPROCITY THEORY OF LOVE

If you are following my thinking thus far and I am still making sense to you, then let us look at some further conclusions we can draw from what this theory actually means. You will see, I think, that there are some fascinating observations that come from accepting the basic premises of the theory. I warned you before that the theory looks harmless, but when you pursue the significance of these observations to their logical conclusions, the results can be surprising.

First, the theory sheds light on such questions as whether or not there is puppy love, whether infatuation is a distinct condition different from love, and whether love at first sight has any basis in fact.

When we use the expression "puppy love," we generally refer to the strong feelings children have for one another or perhaps for an adult. The use of the word "puppy" implies that this love is not a very serious one; it is cute, but it is not long-lasting, not deep, and is based only on the flimsiest considerations. And whatever else a person may say about it, the common thinking has it that puppy love is certainly not "true" love.

I take complete exception to this view. Puppy love is a powerful emotion that arises out of the expectations and experiences of one person with another. The child generally anticipates that a friend or an adult will satisfy his or her deepest desires and needs. If that is what this person is anticipating and those feelings of satisfaction result, then how can that differ in any way from the feeling that you have for your husband or wife? Puppy love can be exquisitely deep and sincere, and just as painful when it breaks up as any adult romance. True, sometimes these romantic attachments last only a short while, and children can sometimes recover in a day or two from a broken love affair. But so can adults. I agree that mature judgment is lacking in a case of puppy love and that the child is fantasizing possibilities that an adult might recognize as totally impractical. So the worst that you can say about this situation is that the child is being foolish, impractical, and blind. But you cannot say that he or she is not in love.

"Infatuation" is the usual term applied when two adults love each other superficially and fleetingly. I think we do such persons a serious disservice when we don't take their experience seriously and don't recognize it as a very powerful love feeling. A couple who have been married happily for fifty years love each other for much the same reasons as do two people who have fallen in love rapidly and who may be blinded by their passions. For those who have just started a passionate relationship, the claim that they are in love is validated in the same way that it is for us all, namely, each is convinced that the other person will satisfy his or her deepest desires and needs. The fact that they may be wrong is only sad. It does not alter their feelings that each is now on the verge of a beautiful existence with another person.

We supposedly run into cases of infatuation where middle-aged adults fall in love precipitously with the strangest partners. The forty-year-old male who suddenly wants to run off with a younger woman with several children but can find no fault with his own wife or family is, in the minds of some people, suffering from an infatuation. If by infatuation we mean he was unwise in his behavior, that he overreacted to a tender relationship, and that he cannot see the forest for the trees, then I would agree that he is suffering from infatuation. However, to claim for one moment that he does not have very powerful feelings for the other woman is to deny what all love feelings are like. If we are going to label as infatuations all middle-age love relationships not based on rational considerations, then we had better refer to ninety-five percent of all marriages as infatuations! Most marriages were initiated at a younger age when there was much less rational control.

"Love at first sight" is a special class of infatuation. It is a powerful feeling that sometimes strikes an individual who has not even been introduced to the object of affection. When you see a stranger across a crowded room and you fall in love at long range, you are obviously the world's champion risk taker. You are concluding with only the flimsiest of evidence that the person across the room has the capacity to make you a happy human being. Perhaps he or she moves right, laughs right, dresses right, looks good; and on those pleasant but not terribly significant considerations you are making a prediction about what that person can do for you.

This love-at-first-sight phenomenon is every bit as genuine, sincere, and valid a love experience as is puppy love, infatuation, or the love between a couple married forty years. It is simply based on an expectation that one's deepest desires and needs can be fulfilled by that other person. Sometimes these hunches work out amazingly well. Sometimes they are complete fiascos. I suspect the latter result happens more often than the former.

Another insight that arises out of the reciprocity theory of love is that you have every right in the world to expect your mate to change in any way that it takes to satisfy your deepest desires and needs. Though you might have married a partner with a set of habits that pleased you five years ago, do not apologize at this point for saying that you do not like these habits anymore and that some of them have to change. If the person comes back and reminds you that you married him or her for better or for worse, your response can always be that you can't accept those particular behaviors anymore because you are unhappy with them. If you are accused of always wanting your partner to change, admit it. The only reason you are complaining is that you want to be happy. You did not marry only to make someone else happy. You also married to make yourself happier. The focus is always upon your own reasonable happiness, first and foremost. Realistically, however, you had better understand that if you want all this happiness for yourself, you have to pay for it. After all, your partner married you for the very same reasons. He or she also wanted greater happiness in life and thought that it could be obtained by marrying you. And your partner obviously understands that in order to achieve greater happiness for himself or herself certain concessions will have to be given to you.

So we are all in this arrangement for the very same

purposes. To suggest that we should not request changes
in our mates is simply nonsense. If behavior exists that we
don't like, are we supposed to accept it graciously? Are we
such fools that we think we must live without complaining
about a situation that brings us misery? When you are
questioned with that age-old statement, "Why can't you
accept me as I am?" you had better respond: "Because I
don't like you that way. It makes me unhappy when you
do those things. I didn't mind those things years ago, but
I've changed and I don't want to tolerate that behavior
anymore."

And why shouldn't you change? As I tried to show in
Chapter 1, we never stay the same; we are always different
people from day to day and from one year to the next.
Anyone who believes that the world stands still, or that
people remain the same as when they met just isn't func-
tioning with all his or her faculties. Expecting new things
from each other is as natural as women loving diamonds
and men loving meat and potatoes. This seems to me to be
such an obvious fact that I marvel when I hear some of my
clients apologize for the pressures they want to put upon
their mates.

If you agree with my definition of love, then you can
easily see my next point: Love must generally be earned.
Only in the cases of infants, pets, and senile parents does
love not need to be earned. In most other instances, that
feeling which we designate as love emerges from us *after*
we have been gratified. It is something that evolves out of
the other person's behavior. Not that it is directly caused
by the other person, but it is a feeling we allow ourselves
to have after someone has proven to us that we are extremely important to him or her. Then we permit the
other's behavior to have a very positive effect on us.

That is why it is *incorrect* to ask people to give you love.
What you really are asking for is certain behaviors that
please you enormously and that cause you to love the

giver. You don't *get* love, you create it inside yourself *after* your deep desires and needs are met. It is the action that people give us, and it is the feeling that we experience. The person whose desires and needs you gratify creates his or her own feeling of love as a result of your kindness.

The next implication from the reciprocity theory is that love means different things to different people. Just as one man's meat is another man's poison, so too, what is a loving act to one person is not necessarily a loving act to another person. When you want someone to love you, it is extremely important that you try to understand what it takes to make that person happy. You had better not interpret happiness just as you see it, but also consider how the other person defines happiness. A typical example of confusion of desires and expectations arises in the giving of flowers as a sentimental gesture. Men often rebel at the practice of giving women flowers to show their love. And from my point of view, being a man, I can understand completely their rational, brilliant, correct, and practical thinking. Wanting flowers to prove someone's love is obviously ridiculous, because the flowers die in a few days, they are rather expensive, and they require no effort on the part of the person aside from spending money to acquire them. The man who is faithful to his wife, works hard to support her and the family, and permits her the same freedoms that he enjoys, is showing her a hundred times more affectionate and loving behavior than three dozen long-stemmed roses could ever show. At least that is the male argument.

But we are now not talking about what it takes to make the man love her; we are asking what it takes to make her love him. And if she says it's long-stemmed roses, then it's long-stemmed roses, my friend. She may be foolish in this regard. She may be adolescent, romantic, impractical, and a victim of too many gothic novels. That's totally irrelevant. If she wants flowers to prove your love, that's what you had better realize, and that's what you had better give.

It should be obvious by now that one of the most logical conclusions to emerge from the above discussion is that for adults, love must be earned. We may all be able to love our cute French poodles and our parakeets without conditions, but this simply does not apply to adults from whom we expect satisfaction of many of our own desires and needs. This comes perhaps as a very unflattering discovery about human nature. I am sorry if it does, but I did not make human nature. I am only a student of it. The fact that I am describing it does not mean that I approve of it. Yet I strongly suspect that many readers will not take kindly to the claim that love is earned and will protest as one man did when I presented these observations to him. He asked: "Do you mean to say, Dr. Hauck, that I love my wife only because of what she does for me and that I would not love her if she displeased me?" My answer was a decided "Yes," because he had described very accurately exactly the way it is between adults. He may not have realized that his wonderful feelings toward his wife were based on the fact that she was really quite successful in making him a happy man. If she had ever denied him seriously, however, he would have found out in very short order just how much he didn't love her.

The notion of having to earn someone's love is actually not a foreign idea to mature persons. Without being told, they usually appreciate the fact that one has to reciprocate in an interpersonal relationship in order to make the relationship work. It is the immature or the spoiled person who has trouble with this idea. If you are a spoiled or immature person, it hardly occurs to you that you owe people something for their efforts on your behalf. Stop believing you have a right to expect love, justice, a job, security, and so on. If you get these things, that's wonderful, but you may be just plain lucky. The idea of paying one's mate back for every effort he or she makes is simply very foreign to the immature person. You can use this observation as a way of determining very quickly if your partner is mature or not. If he or she is always raising the roof when you ask for a reasonable favor, although you have knocked yourself out for him or her, then you have a child on your hands. People who (a) think things always have to go their way and (b) become bitter, angry, or resentful when things do not go their way are by definition immature persons. If you are engaged to such an individual, I am inclined on rational grounds to tell you to break off the engagement. These people are not easy to live with; and it will take them quite a while to grow up, often at your expense and as a result of many efforts on your part. If you believe that you do not want to spend your time making someone else grow up, then go look for a more mature mate right now.

Frequently I hear my clients say, "I hate it when my mate uses me," or "I feel very guilty when I think I am using my mate." The idea that we use each other in a loving relationship seems to be so unacceptable and un-flattering that people automatically want to deny it or stop doing what they are doing if they conclude that they are in fact being used or doing the using. And yet, is this not what is actually happening between all people who love each other? Of course we use each other. If I have desires and needs that I cannot satisfy by myself, I am obviously interested in a relationship with another human being—because it is the other human being who can satisfy those desires and needs for me. So I am using that person's skills, interests, talents, financial resources, looks, or whatever I need, in order to make myself a happier person. And the same goes in the other direction. You are being used because of certain advantages you can give the other person, things that will make that individual happier. There are very few relationships that are not somehow reciprocal in nature. The only time a relationship is not based on reciprocity is when one person is doing all the giving and getting nothing in return. If you help someone who is powerless to do you a favor, or to pay you for your services, or to help you in any way at all, then that is a nonreciprocal relationship and is the one exception to the rule of our using each other. If you want to be a good Samaritan and pick up injured persons on the highway, take them to the nearest hospital, see to it that they are taken care of, and then drive off like the Lone Ranger without waiting for thanks or recognition, more power to you. Just being of service is apparently all the reward you need. But that again refers to the fraternal love I spoke of before. When a relationship becomes more intense and is based on very frequent contacts, we all become somewhat self-interested and do not want to give endlessly. We expect to receive as well as give.

Let us stop feeling guilty over the fact that we use each other. Of course we do. I use my secretaries for their skills and my secretaries use me for the salary that they earn. I use my grocer because he gives me vegetables, and I give him dollars. We use our mates for a hundred different services, and they expect a hundred back. To suggest, therefore, that you are cheap and degraded because you are only staying with someone to use him or her is absurd.

THE BUSINESS THEORY OF MARRIAGE

Marriages are made by two individuals who have made the judgment that they have a higher-than-average degree of compatibility and can please each other to such an extent that institutionalizing the relationship seems only logical. Why let a person you admire just float in and out of your life when, with effort and commitment, that relationship could flower into a lifelong partnership? So, rather than simply shake hands on the deal and flip a coin to decide who will move in with whom, people—as civilization has become more complex—have created the institution of marriage. This makes the two lovers aware of the fact that they have committed themselves to each other, that they have certain legal obligations to each other that normally do not exist until they are married, and that their relationship now has the backing and the approval of society, their personal friends, and the lawcourts themselves. It is a serious business because, in most cases, before many years pass it will involve other human beings and an estate —which at times can amount to a fortune. With all this at stake it only makes sense to legitimatize the relationship.

For the woman in particular, it is a critical move. When she agrees to walk down the aisle with her fiancé and to make herself vulnerable to whatever good or bad fortune may come of her husband's efforts to provide for her during periods when she is rather helpless (as during pregnancy, illness, or the rearing of a family), she had better have some guarantees that she will not be abandoned casually during these critical times. If she is going to allow herself to be in the position of giving birth and rearing children, she will certainly want to have reassurance in some form that she will not starve, have to give the children away, or have to go into prostitution to support herself and the children. In this respect she is simply being intelligent, using good judgment, using her head rather than her heart, and facing the reality of what might happen to her if she does not make some hard business decisions.

A man owes a woman this kind of reassurance because, if the two of them want a family, it is so ordained that she will be the one who will carry the child, deliver it, and in most cases rear it. This means that she will have to forgo many of her own career plans, which—if she were not to raise a family for herself and her husband—would at times allow her to have a very interesting life and possibly even allow her to acquire considerable wealth. But being a housewife and homemaker does not always coincide with being able to support oneself in a reasonable style. That is an unspoken agreement the couple make when they get married and decide to have a family. Therefore, she has as much right to his income as he has, because she forfeited her opportunity for an independent wage when she decided to please them both by having a family. It is entirely unfair for a man to expect his wife to give him a family, to give up her own career, and then to insist that the money he makes is entirely his, when there is no other way he could have had a family. It surprises me how many women do not understand their rights to the husband's earnings because of that fact. I have talked to hundreds of women who do not know how much their husbands earn, or how much is in the checking account, and who have no say in the purchase of the next car. They accept the fact that, because the husband actually did the work, the money is his and the wife must be content to rely on his sense of generosity to let her have enough for a dress or groceries. This is chauvinism at its worst. And too many women abide by it.

A woman in this condition does not give herself the credit she deserves. She has every right to equal control over the family funds for two more reasons. The first is that she certainly earns every penny she shares with her husband, because she services his needs and the family's needs in dozens of ways. Most women don't sit at home throwing bonbons into their mouths and getting fat while they watch television all day. The average housewife works hard, handles a multitude of responsibilities, and often lives a lonely and boring life that would drive the husband nuts if he tried it for three days. Any husband who doesn't believe this ought to take a two-week vacation at home while his wife goes off someplace. In a great many instances the man finds out just what it is like to care for children, pets, laundry, cooking, and keeping the house shipshape just so she won't gripe when she comes home.

The next reason why women have a right to equal control over the funds is that they are the blue-collar workers of the family, and unless they strike once in a while, their deep desires and needs will be completely ignored. Isn't it odd that the same man who walks the picket line on strike against the factory that employs him, and that will not recognize his reasonable demands, will go home and take the role of management in his own house and strenuously reject offers from his wife that she makes in the role of laborer. It does seem as though what we regard as right or wrong depends largely on whether we are asking or giving.

However this may be, it is extremely important that you begin to look upon marriage as a business arrangement between two people who had better get a fair amount of happiness from the business if they don't want it to collapse. A factory can only succeed if both management and labor are getting a fair share of the benefits, and a marriage can only succeed if the same conditions are met. Try to see marriage as a business arrangement between two partners joining forces with each other, rather than between an employer and an employee. Marriage is like a company called Smith & Smith, whose objective is happiness. Achieving happiness in a marriage is the equivalent of turning a profit in a business. Being unhappy is like being in the red, having more debts than you can pay. The similarities between a marriage and a business go on. In the business world, if you don't like your job, you might abruptly quit it. In marriage that's called desertion. If you want to leave your job permanently, you resign or get fired. In a marriage that's called a divorce.

Every business starts out with a list of job specifications that describe in some detail what it will take to make that job succeed. Every employer notifies new employees of the times they are expected to be on the job, the kind of work they will be expected to do, the number of sick days they will have, when they will get their first vacations, and so on. This is essential so that future confusion will be avoided.

Would that it were so with marriages. Couples seal themselves into a contract more binding than many conditions of employment, and they don't even realize it. Every husband and every wife expects certain benefits, favors, behaviors, and treats to come from the partnership in the months and years ahead. So does every employer and employee. The employee expects certain work conditions, promotions, raises, and fringe benefits. Usually no one marries another person without some expectation of reciprocity.

It is my observation that couples who spell out the conditions of their marriage beforehand often have less difficulty than those that do not. And aren't they acting like business people when they do this? If a man and a woman decide that they will put money away every month to buy a house, that they will have a family started no later than three years after the marriage, that they will alternate spending Christmas at each other's parental homes, and so on, they will usually encounter fewer frustrations than the couple who have made no such plans.

A marriage and a business handle frustrations in very similar ways. If an employer is unhappy with an employee, he or she notifies the employee and makes a suggestion that the tardiness be corrected, that the employee spend less time on breaks away from the job, or that the work be done more carefully. In a marriage, husband and wife also have frequent conversations describing their mutual frustrations and how they would like to see them altered. He wants her to keep the house a bit cleaner. She wants him to give a little bit more of his time to the children.

If these discussions do not achieve their end, the employer becomes more harsh with the difficult worker. The boss may now speak louder, become quite blunt, threaten some kind of suspension, or dock the worker's pay, and may make it more strongly known that he or she is running out of patience because of the worker's unacceptable performance. Husbands and wives do the same thing. They will begin to yell and argue to make their feelings more strongly known. Then he may realize that she does not want sex four times a day, and she may understand that he must have one day at the golf course with the boys.

If an employer finds that stern warnings do not work, he may suspend the worker for a few days or may move him or her to a less satisfying position. Husband and wife can also take time off from each other for a few days. She may go to her mother's. He may stay at the club. Or if they had just been planning to go on a trip together, one of them may now cancel.

If the difficult worker does not change the undesirable behavior significantly at this point, the boss may simply give him or her walking papers or ask for a resignation. In marriage this is equivalent to a separation or a divorce. If these similarities between business and marriage don't impress you, then consider the fact that both undertakings involve huge sums of money and that legal measures are required to begin or to end them. For hundreds of years marriage was not primarily a matter of love at all but an agreement to cement governments, countries, or tribes. It was strictly a business arrangement in which cattle were offered or dowries were expected.

You don't like the idea that your marriage is a business arrangement? Frankly, I don't like it either. I wish I had not come to that conclusion. But what choice did I have? When you take away all the hearts and flowers, you are left with a pretty hard-nosed business arrangement. And if you don't believe that, you should just hear some of my

clients talk about how they are going to take the husband
or wife to the cleaners once they get them into the court-
room. And what do you think they are going to fight over
in court? Custody of the children, support payments, alimony, and how to divide up the furniture, the house, and
the car. That's not a bingo game, ladies and gentlemen,
that's hard finance.

The notion of marriage being a loving business may be
harder for men to accept than for women. I have a hunch
that women have always seen marriage as a business arrangement about which they had better be quite practical. That hasn't been the case with men. That's why I feel
the male is by far the more romantic of the two. When he
falls in love he actually does not consider the relationship
as a business as much as the female does. I am not praising
the male over the female when I say this; I am only making
an observation.

For example, this is why men fall in love much more
quickly than women. In considering his proposal to marry,
the man usually thinks of sex, having a home and family.
He likes her looks and her figure, and she seems reasonably easy to get along with. What other considerations
does the man *need* to think of when he makes a proposal?
He usually isn't going to ask himself whether she can support him. At least that's not the way it has been for hundreds of years. He isn't going to ask himself whether she
would desert him if he should become handicapped or
disabled. Young men don't think they can ever die, much
less be incapacitated, and of course they don't get preg-
nant. In short, he doesn't want a lot *from* her. He wants
her. He'll supply the rest for himself.

For the woman it is quite another matter. She is a fool
if she does not think of the marriage in very practical and
businesslike terms. Most parents accept this in regard to
their daughters. If a girl brings home a young man in
whom she is interested, what is the first thing her parents

want to know about him? They of course want to know
what he looks like, what he acts like, and whether he is a
man of character and intelligence or a knucklehead. And
they certainly want to know his educational background,
his work experience, the extent of his skills, and how responsible and hardworking he is. Why are those questions
asked of the male much more than of the female? Because
he is usually the one expected to bring home the money.
He will earn the living while the woman will sooner or
later bear children and have to stay home to care for them.
Even though there are women who do a better job of
supporting their husbands than vice versa, or who are able
to have a career and children at the same time, my statement is true on the average for most of the women
throughout the world. They become dependent on the
man's skill for bringing home the bread and the bacon. It
is therefore incumbent upon them (and very wise besides)
to look him over very carefully, not just for his sex appeal,
but to determine what kind of father he is going to be, if
he is going to be a considerate husband, whether he is
going to be a drunk, and whether he is going to be able to
provide her with the kind of living she enjoys. This is why
the men who make the most money, who show the most
promise, and who have the best education become the
most eligible bachelors.

Think of two contests, one featuring the most desired
bachelors in a city, and one featuring the most eligible
single women. What are we thinking of when we think of
each? Are we going to judge both by the same standards?
Of course not. The most eligible bachelor is going to be
someone who is loaded with dough and dripping with
charm, who dresses like a fashion plate and looks like a
movie star, but, most of all, who can give a woman the
life-style that she has always dreamed of. It's great, of
course, if he happens to be as handsome as a movie star,
but that isn't the biggest drawing card as far as women are

concerned. He may be bald-headed and not particularly good looking, but if he is a charming guy and has great financial security, that will make up for what he lacks in physical appearance.

But the most eligible single woman has to have curves all in the right places, a lovely head of hair, and white pearly teeth, look like a model for a beer ad, and then have the right personality and character. She doesn't have to have wealth. If she is attractive and enjoys being made love to, she has practically won him over.

That's why I say it is the man who tends to be the romantic. His heart and soul are focused on the physical and social pleasures the woman can give him. Her focus is just as often on the material advantages she can get from him, along with what she feels for him personally. She is the practical one; the man is the dreamer.

A word of caution, and a word of defense. I am not criticizing women because of this. I accept it as reality, and I am not making a judgment about it. Nor am I saying that the man always remains more romantic than the woman. Actually, after the honeymoon it often turns out that he loses much of his romanticism while she gains more. The tables are turned: she often winds up craving him on a personal level much more than he craves her, and he finally desires more material things and wants to be with others more than with his wife.

Just after writing the above remarks I met my next client, a woman who was living with a man with whom she had just had an argument. She was dependent upon him financially; so it was quite a shock when he asked her to pack up her bags and leave his home. My client was capable of dealing with this sudden reversal and had some means by which she could survive the temporary hardship. However, she pointed out (without my asking) that she could now understand why women want to be brides rather than mistresses. As she put it: "There is simply no protection for the woman if she breaks up with the fellow. At least if she's married, she has child-support rights and shares in his estate, insurance benefits, and perhaps alimony. At my age that makes a whale of a lot of difference when a relationship ends as suddenly as mine just did."

I wondered why she hadn't figured this out years ago, since she was a perfectly intelligent woman. I had to conclude that she was basically one of those romantic types, much like the men I've been describing. She had lost the sense of practicality that most of her sisters have, and this experience made her realize again what love and marriage are truly all about.

Do you begin to understand why I called marriage a loving business? Is it still so difficult to see a marriage as an agreement similar to any other contract? Unless the terms of the contract are met, the relationship, no matter what kind it is, will be broken. I contend therefore that those marriages which are run like efficient businesses are more likely to develop romance and last longer than those which start out being purely romantic, never become practical, and wind up with the couple being disturbed, hysterical, and angry and wondering what the devil happened to their wonderful dreams.

HEALTHY REASONS FOR MARRYING

If you accept my thesis that people marry in order to have a reasonable degree of satisfaction of their deep desires and needs, then the next important question we want to ask ourselves is: Just what are those deep desires and needs for which we marry?

In my experience there are about four healthy reasons why we marry and about nine unhealthy reasons. I shall go over these points briefly, but anyone wishing to study this material more fully can consult my book *Marriage Is a Loving Business.*

The healthy and mature reasons for marriage are:

Companionship

A mate should be your best friend. He or she is someone with whom you can talk over practically anything. He or she is someone with whom you can gladly be alone for hours on end. He or she is someone with whom you simply feel as comfortable as an old shoe. Why would anyone want to give up such a person and let him or her enter and exit your life without trying to hold on permanently? When you have a good friend, you do whatever you can to cultivate the friendship and to be in the company of that friend for as many hours as you desire.

A Safe and Convenient Sex Life

This reason for marrying certainly should not be frowned upon. A safe and convenient sex life is one of the unique contributions that a loving relationship has that other relationships often do not have. Sexual gratification is an integral part of all of our lives, even into the eighties and nineties. Most people marry with the full expectation that the relationship will bring forth pleasant and satisfying sex. Great stress is almost certain to result in the absence of sexual fulfillment.

If you have been true to your oath and have been faithful—both of you—the whole question of venereal diseases need never arise. In this day and age of herpes, a disease for which there is no known cure, who wants a sex life with a series of partners one of whom is likely to give you such an infection?

A safe and sane sex life is also more likely with a couple who are married and who work out their sexual problems than it is with individuals who switch partners every few days or months. It takes time to work out our sexual styles. But once our preferences have been communicated and our mate is used to them, we have created a situation in which we are comfortable with our partner's lovemaking.

Raising a Family

Different societies and even modern-day governments have attempted to alter the traditional method of rearing a family. The Chinese have in some instances developed communal arrangements for the rearing of the young, while the Israelis have the kibbutz. From my reading on this subject I believe that these are not great improvements over conventional methods of rearing our children. In some instances, a child might become more independent and not suffer the problems of living with a disturbed parent if the child is separated earlier and for greater periods of time, as in a state school or in a kibbutz. However, given a normal set of parents, there still seems to be no other method that truly equals the care, devotion, and end results we humans get when we raise our children ourselves.

Those of us who have had pleasant childhoods can easily explain them on the basis of having loving memories of brother and sisters, mothers and fathers, uncles and aunts, all of whom worked together to provide us with security, love, and recognition.

In the kibbutz the children were separated from their parents for the greater part of the day and slept in large rooms with other children under the care of an elderly adult. If the child had a nightmare, it was another child who consoled him or her. Mother and father were off in another cabin. No doubt this led to considerable self-sufficiency. Whether it led to stronger and healthier people remains to be adequately demonstrated.

Leaving aside the argument of positive effects on the children, raising a family also provides great pleasure and growth-promoting experiences for the parents. To become a parent is to relive your own life. To sacrifice for children teaches you patience, endurance, and understanding. It may be wonderful for children to be raised by parents, but it is equally healthy for parents to have children they enjoy raising to maturity. The whole process is an experience that leads to growth, maturity, and fulfillment.

A Unique Life-Style

The life a woman will lead depends in large measure on the man she marries and the occupation he has. This is not to say that his life is not influenced by the woman he marries. Obviously each will have an enormously important effect upon the other. A woman who marries a college professor will have a very different life than she would have if she married a physician or a bricklayer.

The life-style a couple will lead depends largely on their earnings, their educational backgrounds, and their social skills. One of my clients, whom I shall call Rose, married a charming salesman who does a lot of traveling. Since neither wanted children, they can and do travel together, spend time at faraway resorts, invariably eat at the finest restaurants, and dress in the latest fashions. She loves this kind of life, and so does he. She wouldn't think of marrying anyone but a businessman who wears a white shirt and a tie and who can provide her with other successful men and women as social companions. She has a very nice home on the edge of the city and gets a new car every year or two. All in all, she couldn't be happier.

Unhealthy Reasons for Marrying

There must be dozens and dozens of bad reasons for marrying someone, but it would serve no purpose to go over each one in great detail. Here are the six most common ones.

Fear of Independence

Anyone who marries because he or she is afraid of becoming an independent person marries for the wrong reason. When some young people are about to grow up, to test themselves against the world, to be on their own completely for the first time, they turn tail on this experience and begin to doubt their own ability to support themselves or live by themselves. Then they immediately permit themselves to fall in love. Notice that I use the word "permit." After all, when we fall in love, it is because we have allowed ourselves to have that emotion. This is not something that is forced upon us; it is something we permit, allow, and talk ourselves into when it is convenient for us to have such an emotion. And one of the most convenient times, or so we think, is when we are about to be cut loose from all of the normal supports we have had while growing up.

Is it any wonder, therefore, that high school students often marry shortly before or after graduation? Can we actually believe that some earth-shattering event occurred in the lives of those young people that made it absolutely mandatory that they be married at this particular time? You and I both know that this is not so. Those people get married because they are afraid to be alone. It is because of their excessive dependency, their need to lean on someone stronger than they, that this decision is

made. People who never have had some years of independence come to regret that they married too early.

To Be a Therapist for Your Mate

As you shall see in the coming chapters, one of the
psychological faults that causes a great deal of misery in
marriages is other-pity. It demonstrates itself in the need
some men or women have to marry another person almost
for the sole purpose of being able to cure that person of
some difficulty. A woman may marry a man because he
drinks or gambles; she believes that she loves him so much
that she is going to cure him of this behavior. Or a man
may feel sorry for a woman because she is down and out,
can't handle her children, and is perpetually depressed,
and he may see himself as the knight in shining armor who
is going to take her away "from all that."

Both of these people are making the same serious mistake: they are marrying in order to be a therapist for the
mate. Let me advise you never to do this. It usually doesn't
work. Being the superior one in the relationship and suggesting that your partner is seriously troubled only makes
that person more insecure and resentful about your sense
of superiority. This leads to a backlash in the form of oppo-
sitional behavior, making matters worse.

To Spite Your Parents

There are few times in your life when you are denser
than when you are a teen-ager. You are beginning to enter
adulthood and want to think for yourself. Yet you don't
have enough experience from life to make all the important decisions. This places teen-agers in a bad spot because
they will have to stick their necks out and make a lot of
dumb mistakes before they learn from the school of hard
knocks. Unfortunately, one of the more common occasions

when children decide they are going to start thinking for themselves (rather than let themselves be advised by their parents) is when they consider getting married. Of all the times for them to reject parental advice, this is perhaps the worst. Parents are wrong about a great many things, and I am the first to admit it. But when most parents advise kids not to get married too young, ninety-nine times out of a hundred they're right. However, because adolescents have to feel their oats and prove to themselves and to the world that they are now capable of thinking without parental guidance, they often spitefully go ahead and marry just to prove they can do it. Little do such prospective brides or grooms, when walking down the aisle, realize that they are trying to spite their parents. That is always a bad beginning for a marriage.

Fear of Spinsterhood or Bachelorhood

People frequently act recklessly while under the influence of fear. Those who anticipate that they will have few opportunities for marriage may be so afraid of remaining spinsters or bachelors forever that they will say "yes" to the very first offer without giving due consideration to the merits of the proposal. When desperate for marriage, people clutch for straws and marry almost anyone who will rescue them from what they consider to be the stigma of the unmarried state. As one of my clients once told me: "I would have married anyone who asked me. I thought I was so unworthy that I would have considered myself lucky to get any invitation, much less the one I hoped for." Needless to say, she had an unhappy marriage and eventually was divorced. She had married someone whom she would never in her saner moments have considered as a mate.

Social pressure is another reason why young people are often self-conscious about not marrying. It is regarded as a failure on their part not to be attractive enough or interesting enough to gain a mate. When everyone around them is going down the aisle to the wedding march and they are still living the single life, most of them think that others are probably wondering what's wrong with them. The realization that it is perfectly mature for someone not to marry early in life, or never to marry at all, simply escapes them.

Because You Were in Love

I shall never forget counseling with a young fellow who was considering his third marriage and wasn't twenty-eight years old yet. I couldn't quite understand how he could get in and out of relationships so easily. From our further conversations I concluded that he had an irrational notion and was convinced that if he fell in love with somebody, he had to marry that person.

Falling in love is not the overpowering emotion that romantic literature and folk songs have led us to believe. It is a strong emotion, to be sure, but it is one we talk ourselves into and one we can also talk ourselves out of. Love may be blind, but it is not the most powerful emotion that we experience. We *can* control it and we *can* fall out of love whenever we have a mind to.

To Escape an Unhappy Home

One of the saddest reasons for marrying is, not that you are drawn toward a person, but that you are repulsed by someone else. A young boy or girl who cannot stand life at home will sometimes be attracted to the idea of marriage with such force that practically anyone can satisfy that need. Girls in particular are prone to use marriage as an escape from an unhappy home. Sometimes boys do it too. More often the young men become adventurous and hit the road, join the army, or hitchhike around the country.

I can fully appreciate the need for young people to get away from screaming parents, drunk or abusing fathers, nagging and demanding mothers. However, at times the fire they jump into is worse than the frying pan from which they leaped. Getting married at an early age and out of a sense of desperation is hardly the way to begin a peaceful and secure future. My advice is: If you are in such an intolerable situation that you feel you must leave, then leave. Try to have a job first, or live with a relative, or work for room and board someplace. But don't get married just to escape from home. All of the fears, the angers, the guilt, and the inferiority that you have as a result of living in your intolerable home will go along with you right into the marriage bed. If you think you are going to start off a brand-new relationship with a clean slate, you are absolutely mistaken.

THE COMPATIBILITY TEST

The principal question that you had better keep on asking yourself when you are falling in love with someone and deciding whether or not to marry is, "Are we compatible?" Compatibility means that the two of you are on the same wavelength. What pleases you generally pleases your partner. When you make your partner happy, you find that you are generally happy also. The more compatibility the two of you have, the better you will be able to get along. Keeping your finger on the pulse of your degree of compatibility is as important for your marriage as is stepping on a scale to check your weight in order to keep it within a desired range.

But what guidelines can you use to judge whether you

are compatible or not? Here are three questions for you. If you are compatible with your lover, you will answer all three in the affirmative.

Question No. 1: Does my partner *understand* my deepest desires and needs?

To answer this question, I want you to write out what you feel are the major frustrations caused by your partner's behavior which, if changed, would make you feel considerably more loving toward him or her. Never mind how unrealistic your request might be at this point. Simply jot down what you feel your lover would have to do to make you less frustrated. The rationale behind this move is, of course, to repair any bad feelings between you. If your partner knows what your deep desires and needs are and can satisfy them, then obviously you will be more inclined to love your mate than if you are frustrated by your mate.

Question No. 2: Is my partner *capable* of satisfying my deepest desires and needs?

Some people who are incompatible simply are totally unable to please their partners in any significant way because they just don't have what it takes. If a woman has great artistic interests, loves to go to art galleries, attends the opera, and fills her house with oil paintings, she is probably not going to feel happily married to a man who wants to trap groundhogs, throws darts in the local saloon on Friday nights, and enjoys watching football all Sunday afternoon. These two are simply not going to get along, not because he is a nasty fellow or because they hate each other, but because her interests are so vastly different from his. He may be incapable of satisfying her deep desires and needs to a degree that could bring her happiness.

Question No. 3: Is my partner *willing* to satisfy my deepest desires and needs?

Your lover may *know* what it takes to make you happy, and may be *capable* of fulfilling those desires and needs, but this does not necessarily mean that he or she will in fact *want* to make that effort. One man told me recently that he was fully aware of what his wife expected of him, and he knew that he was also perfectly capable of being the kind of husband she wanted him to be. But it no longer pleased him to be that way and therefore he had to say "no" to this third question.

As I mentioned previously, your partner is compatible with you if he or she can answer these three questions with a "yes." A single "no" answer means that there is a degree of incompatibility that is going to give you trouble. I would suggest that you not get married until the negative answers change to affirmative ones. If you are married, I would certainly urge you to clarify your frustrations and remove them as much as possible. Or get into marriage therapy.

THE GOAL OF ANY CARING RELATIONSHIP

When we come right down to it, the long and the short of rewarding human interaction depends on each party's getting a reasonable amount of satisfaction from the other. You don't go into a job to make the boss happy unless the boss in willing to do something to make you happy. If you will recall my statements about the reciprocity theory of love, you can extend them into broader areas and speak of the reciprocity theory of friendships, or the reciprocity theory of international diplomacy. People are not totally self-sacrificing; they expect some benefit in return. The question is: How much do you have a right to expect? You have a right to be just reasonably content in any voluntary relationship. This is a point of emotional equilibrium that enables you to say that you are feeling fairly good about what's going on between you and your partner, that things aren't half bad, that you're glad you're married or in love, and that although you would still like a great many more things going your way, you can tolerate the situation without resentment if it doesn't get any better than it is. The point at which you can say this to yourself is the point of Just Reasonable Contentment (JRC). The goal of a relationship is to see to it that you remain at least just reasonably content at all times and that you have hope for a greater degree of contentment. When the parties involved can all say that they are reasonably content, there is obviously little reason to complain, and each party is bound to be pleased with the other party.

There are three serious consequences from allowing yourself to live in a state of frustration that is below your JRC level.

The first obvious consequence is that you will generally be a disturbed, unhappy, and frustrated human being. If you are chronically dissatisfied, you are usually going to get depressed, angry, think of infidelity, bite your nails, sleep poorly, drink, or take your frustrations out on the kids. You may use therapy to talk yourself into a reasonable state of calmness; but again, if your frustrations continue, you are simply not going to enjoy life a great deal even though you may not turn into a full-blown neurotic.

The second result of chronically living below your JRC level is that you will most definitely begin to fall out of love with your partner. After all, what is there to be in love about if your partner is continually frustrating you? You have to be a seriously troubled person (and a desperate one besides) in order to continue to love someone who is mistreating you.

This loss of love usually happens rather slowly as the disappointments from one injustice and injury after another begin to pile up over the months and years. If there are not enough times when you are above your JRC level, you eventually are going to fall out of love with your partner. It doesn't matter how much you were in love to begin with; it doesn't matter what your religious faith is; it doesn't matter what your resolve is. Your feelings of love change eventually if you are not getting from your lover a reasonable amount of satisfaction.

Those who feel guilty over falling out of love are misinformed as to what is going on. It is not an evil thing to fall out of love. Falling out of love is no more evil than feeling hungry when you have not been fed. And you don't have to feel guilty over rejecting others for *their* negligence. You are simply acting in a sensible, rational, and healthy way.

The third consequence of living below the JRC level on a chronic basis is that you will eventually not care about the relationship itself. When this happens on the job you eventually tell the boss to take his or her job and keep it. With a marriage you finally come to the conclusion that the whole thing is no longer worth the trouble. You have lost all your feelings, and you say, "I don't have to live like this anymore."

Here, too, a great many people tend to feel guilty when they decide to end a marriage. When a marriage goes sour, and you won't change, it is your *duty* to do something about it. Remember that you are in a marriage, not for the other person's sake, but for your own. You didn't get a job to make your boss happy; you got a job to improve your own life. You enter a marriage, you find a job, you have a friendship, because it serves *your* purposes to have these things. And when they don't do you any good, you wisely want to withdraw from them. If a marriage is simply a waste of time to you, if it is creating great hardships and no longer gives any pleasure, then thoughts of breaking up the marriage are bound to occur to you, and *rightly* so.

You are not doing anyone a favor when you sacrifice yourself for someone else's happiness while at the same time you are becoming a miserable human being. As a matter of fact, you are doing your partner a serious disservice, because you wind up spoiling your mate, frustrating yourself, and getting fed up with your mate. Then one fine day you pack your bags and leave. If you really care so much about a relationship, frustrate it sometimes and train the people around you not to get you to despise them.

Accept the fact that a relationship exists happily because both people are reasonably pleased. When they are not, it is the duty, the moral obligation, of the person who is the most frustrated to do something to relieve the unhappy characteristics of the condition. That is the goal of a relationship: to make yourself reasonably content so that you do not want to end the relationship. To say it in a more practical way, the goal is to push the other party to give in to you repeatedly for favor after favor until you can say to yourself that you are reasonably content. At that point you have serviced yourself and *anyone else* in the *relationship,* and you have done so in a moral and correct way.

3

The Best Ways to Achieve Love

The best attitude to take when you first encounter other people is to assume that they are fairly decent, that they mean you no harm, and that if you treat them well you will be treated fairly in return. That is the essence of Rule No. 1: When someone treats you nicely, reward that behavior as soon as possible by treating that person nicely also.

This is known as positive reinforcement, one of the principles of animal and human learning theory as investigated in psychological laboratories throughout the world. When you reward a behavior, that behavior becomes strengthened. In psychological language we say the behavior is reinforced. Stop and think for a moment what a powerful thing this is if you can use it correctly. If you know what is important to your partner, you can obviously make him or her enormously happy if you reinforce the behaviors that please that person.

Suppose you want your husband to lose weight so he will be more appealing to you sexually. Keep Rule No. 1 in mind when dealing with him day in and day out. If he starts jogging, for example, and you do not make any comments about the jogging, he may lose heart and quit. Or suppose he deliberately pushes aside a serving of dessert and you do not praise him for his willpower. Again you have missed an opportunity to reinforce his dieting behavior. It takes no genius to understand that if you want the man to continue to lose weight, you had better recognize his efforts by mentioning them at the very least.

Although this sounds like simplicity itself, it is actually a complicated subject. There are certain problems not immediately apparent in trying to be a reinforcing individual. Consider some of the following:

What Is a Reward?

We each define for ourselves what a reward is. You must not make the assumption that just because something pleases you enormously it will also please someone else. There are primary reinforcers, such as food, water, sleep, and warmth, that are necessary for physical survival. They are rewards for anyone most of the time. But whether a suit of clothing, a compliment, or a pay raise will serve as a reward depends upon the person who is receiving the reward, the age of the person, the personality of the person, and the particular events in that individual's life at the time the reward is being made. A fur coat is not very impressive to a woman who already has six. Being taken out to a restaurant on his birthday may be the last thing a man wants if he is a traveling salesman and eats out ninety-five percent of the time anyway. A reward for him would be a home-cooked meal.

The Time of the Reward

A reward and its effects depend not only upon the *kind* of reward it is but also *when* it is given. It is important that a person be in a receptive mood for a reward in order for it to have its intended effect. Making a meal for someone when the person is not hungry is simply bad timing. Giving someone a rifle when he is thirty-five years old because he always wanted one when he was fifteen doesn't make sense either. Showing your appreciation by saying "I love you" to your partner may also be badly timed if you are doing so after you have been nagged for a particular favor a dozen times.

THE FREQUENCY OF THE REINFORCEMENT

The effects a reward will have on us obviously depend upon how *often* the reward is made. If you want to influence your lover, it is important not only that you give an appropriate reward, and that you do so at an appropriate time, but also that you do so at a frequency that will have the greatest impact. There are two ways you can reward people: continuously or intermittently. In the first case you are rewarding desirable behavior every time it occurs. Naturally that behavior will become strengthened rather rapidly. If you flatter and praise your partner for each kind act, for each new article of clothing that looks attractive, and each time the partner looks particularly beautiful, a great deal of feeling is bound to be generated toward you because you are being so complimentary. But when you are in the habit of making repeated rewards and then for some reason stop making them, the individual may immediately stop responding.

However, if you use *intermittent* reinforcement, you will compliment only once in a while. When your lover, who has started jogging, does not get a compliment every day, he or she may still exercise repeatedly, even though not being constantly rewarded. Your partner anticipates that the behavior *will* be reinforced in the near future.

Isn't it odd that when we reinforce a habitual behavior on a less-than-constant basis, that habit is harder to break than it would be if we reinforced it one hundred percent of the time?

In summary, let us always be aware that to be loved, one should *(a)* have a good idea of what a reward is for the other individual at this time of life; *(b)* know that the reward interests the person at this time of life; and *(c)* reward often at first, then reinforce on a once-in-a-while basis (intermittently), not every time.

PSYCHOLOGICAL REWARDS MOST VALUED

If you want to be a loving person and get people to love you in turn, it is critical that you think of rewarding behavior in practically all of your dealings with others. Sometimes it is essential that you know what the specific rewards are that appeal most to your lover. In general, however, you cannot go terribly wrong if you know what those behaviors are which simply appeal to most people under most circumstances.

Praise

I cannot emphasize how important praise is in influencing someone's feelings toward you. Most people who are praised for their actions repeatedly wind up with a sense of self-worth, self-confidence, and self-respect. They are not as much affected by mistakes or rejection, because they have been thoroughly programmed to believe that they are decent and worthwhile people. If you want someone to love you, I urge you always to *accentuate the positive* and often to *ignore the negative.* It is almost impossible not to be influenced by someone who is treating you in this lovely and tender fashion.

We simply do not praise each other enough. We rationalize that we are being phony, or that "there aren't that many good behaviors in people to justify constant praise." Sometimes we are afraid we are going to spoil others rotten by pumping them up with too much recognition.

Before I make some comments about these three reasons why people resist giving praise, let me first explain

what I mean by praise. I am referring strictly to complimenting a person on his or her *behavior,* never to complimenting the individual personally. It is essential that we
separate *people* from their *behaviors* and then say something about their actions rather than about themselves.
This is the very best way to give praise, since it does not
evaluate the person either positively or negatively. If this
is done from the earliest years of a child's life, the child
learns never to hate himself or herself because of bad
actions, and correspondingly never feels superior, conceited, or vain because of good actions.

A fundamental irrational philosophy all of us learn as we
grow up is that there are such things in the world as evil,
wicked, or bad people who should be severely punished
and treated harshly to change them into good people. This
is one of those dangerous notions which rational-emotive
therapists have been helping people challenge for years.
The experiences and writings of such advocates of Rational-Emotive Therapy as Dr. Albert Ellis and Dr. Maxie
Maultsby, along with my own, clearly indicate it is a fallacy
to judge people by their actions. When we separate behavior from person, profound changes can take place in the
levels of guilt and inferiority people will suffer. And this
will all be done without—even for an instant—relieving
them of any sense of responsibility whatsoever.

My advice to people who want to be loved and to demonstrate their love is to give praise in huge quantities. Say
nice things to people. We hear those kinds of comments
all too infrequently. People are only too willing to criticize
each other rather than compliment each other. I maintain
that you can compliment just as frequently as you can
criticize. When a thing is done well, why not mention it?
Is your partner punctual? Compliment the punctuality
(but not the person). Say "Thank you" frequently. Get into
the habit of noticing all those nice things that people are
doing for you but that you have been taking for granted.

If your son comes into the house and closes the door behind him, why not praise him for being so thoughtful? Do you protest that this is excessive? Then what would you say if the child came in and left the door ajar? But of course you would call him back, mention it to him, and perhaps even ask him if he was born in a barn. Notice that the issue was not too small to criticize, but it was apparently too small to praise. That is a distinction we seem to make quite often. And that is why I say that if you would praise as often as you criticize, this would be a much better world.

Those who insist they would feel like a phony making numerous compliments are indeed making a bad excuse. Feel like a phony if you must, but don't use that as an excuse for discontinuing the compliments. The feeling of phoniness arises essentially from this being new behavior for you. You also feel like a phony when you go out on the dance floor for the first time, or when you have to give a short speech to your civic club. To complain of feeling phony is nothing more than saying that you are unfamiliar with the task at hand. The more you practice the task, the better your skills become, and the less phony you will feel.

What about spoiling people with compliments? If that actually happened, I would be the first to advise against it. However, as I have already suggested, if you separate your compliments and praise from comments about the person himself or herself, there is no way you can spoil that person. Spoiling people comes from telling them that they are better than others *because* they happen to be better in some particular behavior or action. This is what gives them big heads and turns their noses into the air. If you confine your remarks simply to a person's accomplishments, personality, material goods, talents, or intelligence, you will be separating the person from his or her attributes. That never leads to spoiling, because no one is making comments about the total person.

Charm and Tenderness

How can you dislike someone who is charming, considerate, tender, and genteel? People who are refined, well-bred, polite, and not defensive have to be the most sought after people in the world. What a pleasure it is to be in the company of someone who knows not only what to say and how to say it but also how to listen. Of all the social graces, these are undoubtedly the most highly prized.

If you want to love and be loved, learn to be charming, considerate, and tender. It is like sunshine on ice. Whose resistance and anger can withstand the warmth, the kindness, and the gentleness of an understanding and tender relationship?

I find these traits much more often in women, possibly because by nature or training they are less aggressive than men. But when you see it at all it is a major achievement for civilization.

We have all known such people. They are sought after in greater numbers than the rest of us are. They have such an uncanny knack of making themselves liked that we thoroughly enjoy their company. We readily invite them to our homes, and we always think of them with a smile. Those individuals of whom I personally have been most fond have consistently been gentle, polite, considerate, and gracious. Try as I might, I simply find it too difficult to hold grudges against them in view of the overwhelming good feelings always generated in their company.

To love and be loved, learn these critical social techniques. But how can this be done? I have thought about this problem for quite some time and have concluded that the primary stumbling block against being a genteel individual is defensiveness. It is not so difficult to be a considerate and cooperative human being if you are not defensive. Defensiveness means that you are out to prove that you are always right and that the other person is wrong and therefore must be shown up as being mistaken. I think people who are only too eager to point out your failings are a pain in the neck. They do not hesitate to find the weak spots in a person's character. To get a compliment out of them is like trying to separate a miser from his gold.

The undefensive person is more interested in keeping a relationship smooth than in being right. If a husband has made a statement with which his wife cannot agree, she does not hesitate to correct him. But if he will not accept that correction, she maintains that she still thinks she is right but could be mistaken and lets the matter rest there. What a nice thing to do! She has asserted herself, she has spoken her piece, and she is willing to let well enough alone because the whole issue is not worth fighting over.

Defensive people are, first and foremost, fearful people. They fear not being perfect. Having to admit being wrong is an embarrassment to them. As a matter of fact, they are embarrassed by a good many things: showing tenderness, saying "I love you," hugging their children, complimenting others, and watching others succeed.

To be a loving person, be fearless. Challenge your irrational belief that you are no good if you're imperfect. Challenge the irrational belief that you are inferior if others are superior to you in certain respects. Stop making mountains out of molehills and then focusing neurotically on your imagined disasters.

It is not the end of the world if you are repaid for your compliment with a lukewarm response. It will not kill you if your child wiggles out of your hug to run off to play. Show the affection anyway. Overcome your fears. If you will stop talking yourself into having them, and try hard to talk yourself out of having them, it will get easier and easier for you to show your affection.

Unless you overcome your fear of intimacy and tenderness you will miss a great many opportunities to reward people for their good behaviors. This will tend to weaken those good actions toward you and leave you the loser. To achieve cooperation, respect, and love by the three rules in this book, you will need to overcome certain emotional problems that hinder each method. For example, the first rule says: If someone does something good to you, do something good to that person. This will not work if you are *afraid* to be good, tender, or complimentary.

A note for the men: I sometimes ask women what they find so appealing and attractive about a particular man whom many of them seem to like. Practically always the women who are particularly fond of a specific man say that he is charming, tender, and considerate. It makes little difference what he looks like, or how much money he has, or how well he dresses. I am convinced that most women like a man who is undefensive, knows what he believes, and is willing to defend his viewpoint, but who readily gives in if it looks as if bad feelings will be generated over an insignificant issue. These are the fellows who get all the respect and attention from the ladies, and it is a lesson I strongly urge all men to think about.

DEEP DESIRES AND NEEDS

In providing people with the rewards it takes to make them love you, nothing could be more important and pertinent than fully understanding their deepest desires and needs. These are the foundation stones of the love relationship you are trying to establish. It is my contention that if you are a complimenting, charming, and tender person, you will undoubtedly get your partner to feel very positive about you. However, to make your lover want to marry you, to live with you for the rest of his or her life, it is necessary not only that you be gracious and considerate but that you have intimate knowledge of that individual's deepest desires and needs. Then, if you can satisfy those deep desires and needs to a *reasonable degree*, you will cause that person to be very fond of you. I specifically used the expression *deep* desires because the mere satisfaction of shallow desires does not lead to marriage. To fall deeply in love we must deal with deepest desires, not just surface desires.

Therefore, in order to be as rewarding as possible to your partner, discuss his or her deep desires and needs at some length. What is it that he wants from you? What is it that she wants? Talk these expectations over or write them down so you will not forget them. And every few months and years conduct that same discussion and check with each other to see whether some new deep desires or needs have cropped up and whether some of the old ones have faded away. Whenever I see a couple in therapy I almost invariably make a list of each person's deep desires and needs so that we can understand what it takes to make the marriage work. Unless we have such information, we have no idea what efforts each person must make. If you are like most people, you have only vague impressions of what your lover wants from you, and your lover has the same vague impressions of what it is that makes you happy. It is not until you write down these desires and needs and discuss them that you can get an idea of what the conditions are that will make this relationship a successful one.

AREAS OF CONFLICT

Even if two individuals do understand each other's deepest needs and desires, frustrations and conflicts are bound to arise. Bear in mind, however, that, although there are several or even many frustrations you would like to see your partner remove, it is still possible for you to be happy together if only one or several *major* items are improved significantly. We cannot expect to get everything we want, even though we deserve it. Where an issue is not terribly important, you may be able to give in to your partner and ignore that matter. However, if an extremely important desire is frustrated and you would feel cheated if you gave in completely, I suggest that you learn to compromise. If you do give in for that one, make sure you get your way almost totally on another issue. These negotiations are not different from labor and management attempts to prevent a strike. All parties want to get enough satisfactions out of the negotiations so they can live with the new contracts. Marriage is a loving business, and, in my view, to make it work we often have to sit around the table and negotiate our various expectations with the same bargaining principles that labor and management use. Keeping all this in mind, let us look more closely at several conflict areas.

Financial Responsibility

When my clients complain about the way their partners handle money, they generally refer to spending too lavishly, not balancing the checkbook properly, making unilateral decisions on expensive items, not consulting with the mate, or being very tightfisted. Women often complain about their husbands wanting to control the purse strings and making them come to him with hands out for grocery money, clothes, or physical checkups for the kids. I am continually surprised at how many women have no idea how much money the husband makes in a year, what his weekly take-home pay is, or what the balance in the checkbook is.

Men, on the other hand, sometimes complain that women have a cavalier attitude about money, treating it as though it grows on trees. And when a woman is unhappy with the amount of money her husband brings home, she may suggest in a rather naive way that he has to bring home more. Men complain that women, because they have often not been out in the working world, do not appreciate economic realities. A man cannot bring home more just because his wife wishes it. The paycheck is an item often beyond a man's control and can only be improved with gradual raises over a long period of time.

Children

Differences over rearing and disciplining children can be one of the most stressful and powerful forces creating difficulty with your mate. And this is understandable. Whether your children are being raised according to your ethical and moral standards or not is certainly not an insignificant issue. It is one of the most important matters that will confront any couple.

Discipline, moral values, religion, self-discipline—these are all among the important characteristics parents want to develop in their children and over which they have some serious differences. A well-organized man who tends to be consistent and who is not afraid to be firm with his children, even though they may temporarily dislike him, may quickly lose respect for his wife if she is a wishy-washy mother. By the same token, a mother who has gentle and loving feelings for her children will be absolutely repelled by a husband who shakes his kids, yells at them, and screams at them because they won't clean up three cents worth of catsup on their plates. She will wind up hating him thoroughly because of his rigidity. Never underestimate the amount of distaste and disgust you can have for your partner if you don't respect that person as a mother or father to your children. That is why I urge you always to talk over your child-rearing practices and try to arrive at some consensus that you can live with.

THE BEST WAYS TO ACHIEVE LOVE   83

Sex

The nature of the sexual relationship between a couple
in love is absolutely critical to the survival of that relationship. Generally the feature that distinguishes a marriage
relationship from a friendly relationship is the addition of
the sexual element. Lovers are friends who sleep together.

Among the sexual desires and needs that men report
most often in psychotherapy are the following wishes: (1)
to have more sex, (2) for the female to take the initiative
more often, (3) for her not to require constant reassurances of his love through small acts of affection or repeated
verbal declarations that he loves her.

Women also have a number of sexual preferences, and
if their lovers could fulfill these, it would make them a
great deal happier with their men. Generally, women do
not like crudeness or bluntness. They like their sex clothed
in softness. They want most sexual words to be words of
love, not of sex. The raw expressions men often use are
generally not appreciated. Women may sometimes use
those profanities when they are angry, but when they are
trying to be romantic and loving, they want to use the
language of the poets, not the language of the street.

Women also like to take their time with their lovemaking. The wham-bam-thank-you-ma'am syndrome almost
universally turns them off. This is because women respond
more slowly and simply cannot get aroused with the rapid-
ity that is common among men.

Another major complaint women have is that they are
expected to make love to their partners after an angry
scene. It totally bewilders them that men want to take
them to bed after they are called sluts and whores and
other assorted vulgarities. Women make love with their
hearts far more than with their bodies, and if the feeling
is not right, the sex is not right. I am absolutely convinced
that if a man wants to be a great lover, he had better learn

how to carry on his sex life with a great deal of affection. Women want the whole thing done correctly, not in some crude, disgusting fashion that treats their bodies as a piece of meat that is there to serve the lustful desires of an animal. I know of few things that turn women off more than the refusal to understand this point. Women seem not to be interested so much in quantity of sex as in quality of sex.

Church and Religion

Oddly enough, people don't have as much conflict with each other over churchly or religious issues as one might anticipate. It seems as though there is a selective factor operating rather nicely before they get married that often precludes these conflicts. People who believe in God usually marry persons who have the same belief. Agnostics will gravitate toward agnostics, and atheists toward atheists.

The most frequent complaint married couples give me concerning church and religious matters is the desire on the part of one of the partners to go to church more frequently as a family. Sometimes it is the mother who sees to it that the children have religious education, and sometimes it is the father. But neither of them wants to take sole responsibility. However, even if there is a strong desire for family church activity and that desire is not met, this is seldom a major cause of stress between the two.

More trouble is caused by serious ethical and religious differences. When mother and father, for example, do not agree over such things as the existence of a God or the need to be accountable to a God, these serious issues can make living with one another rather strained. This is not always true, of course; I have known many couples who had vastly different religious backgrounds on the day they were married. True to expectation, they had their ups and downs regarding these religious differences; but in many cases they adjusted to one another's views or decided to put religious issues aside and not let them interfere with the rest of their lives.

The ethical issues are every bit as serious as the religious. Divergent views on lying, stealing, and other moral issues are profoundly disruptive to a marriage. They are so powerful, in fact, that compromise may not be possible. This difference sets the ethical issues apart from other conflict areas, which are usually negotiable.

Relatives and In-Laws

Problems with relatives and in-laws may be infrequent, but when they exist they exist with intensity. The issue is usually the interference of relatives and in-laws in the marriage. Perhaps the husband is too closely tied to his parents and values their opinions over those of his wife. Or a wife can be so dominated by her mother and spend so much time over at her home that the husband feels he is not number one in her life.

Devotion to Work

There are a number of ways in which the job of the husband or wife can interfere with marital happiness. Women complain the most about the devotion their partners show toward jobs. They often feel as though they are second to a man's profession or occupation. Men frequently bring work home, readily accept overtime assignments, and may even busy themselves with chores around the house to such an extent that the women often feel ignored, rejected, and lonely.

A particular kind of work can also be a significant frustration in a marriage. Physicians are called on at all hours of the night. Their meals are interrupted, they are frequently not available for family holidays, and they often have rounds to make on Saturdays and Sundays. Any woman who marries a physician and is not ready to accept that kind of life-style is blind and foolish.

Being married to a truck driver or to a musician also has its built-in frustrations for the female. People in these occupations generally do a lot of traveling, or they work almost exclusively in the evenings—times when the wife would most like to have a man around the house. Some men work on the second or third shift in large factories, and this too can be a source of enormous frustration. It becomes even worse if the wife happens to be working a different shift.

In the same category of work and occupation is the frustration that women have over being just homemakers. Not infrequently they want to go back to school so that they can get a better job and do something more than sit around waiting for the kids to come home from school. This is sometimes a frightening experience for the woman, because she will have been out of school for years and may not remember how to add fractions or take notes for a history course. Sometimes, however, the biggest obstacle she runs into is the reluctance of her chauvinistic husband to agree to let her further her education. Insecure men find ambitious women quite threatening. Not only are they sometimes afraid that their wives are really smarter than they are; they also fear what would happen if their wives were to advance professionally, make good money, or socialize at the managerial level while the men remain at the laboring level. Furthermore, husbands are sometimes frightened by their wives' wanting to stop off with their friends at a cocktail lounge to socialize a bit.

Another difficulty arising out of work is that the man sometimes feels he has no obligation to help around the house because he puts in his eight hours in the factory. He is free, in his mind, to go bowling, hunting, golfing, or drinking because he has done his share. Women, of course, deeply resent this because in no way do they believe that putting in eight hours on a job frees them from any other family obligations. This is a macho idea that is going to have a hard time dying. If a man wants the love of his wife, however, he had better be aware of her bitterness over his thinking that his eight hours of work is somehow more important than her eight hours. And her objection will be that for her it isn't just eight hours; it's more like twelve or fourteen.

SOCIALIZING

In talking to troubled couples, I am surprised at how often both parties want to have more social life. This seems to be a difficult thing for many of them to achieve. Sometimes one of the couple has good social skills and seems to arrange all the social functions. The other is happy to follow along but often cannot be the initiator who meets the people or makes the suggestions for a social get-together. I find that those marriages which have a fair amount of social life in them are among the happier ones. It gets to be pretty boring simply going to a movie with the kids or with your partner week after week. Many couples who otherwise would be terribly bored at home can cure that simply by knowing that on Friday night, Saturday night, or Sunday afternoon something is cooking and they will be attending a party or a small dinner, or just taking a drive with another adult couple. The couple that socializes together stays together.

IRRITATING AND ANNOYING HABITS

Ask yourself if your mate has irritating and annoying habits that seem trivial on the surface but can be so annoying to you at times that you could start a fight over them. Among the examples that I have come across in my practice are: people squeezing saliva through their teeth and making hissing noises; others sniffing all the time rather than using a handkerchief. I have come across a great many women who object to their husbands telling obscene jokes in polite company or using profanity in inappropriate settings.

Annoying or irritating habits are usually not so serious as to cause a marriage to break up. If several bad habits exist, however, and if they are offensive enough, they can be every bit as serious as some of the other objections we have studied.

A FEW CAUTIONS

To give you a better idea of what some people consider serious frustrations in a marriage, let me go through my records for a moment and pick out some of the objections my clients have expressed, or would like to express, to their husband or wife:

1. Think of me as a capable individual, not someone you need to yell at all the time.
2. Tell me where you go when you leave the house.
3. Include me in the financial matters in the family.
4. Make the children more responsible by being more consistent with the penalties you set for them.
5. Tell me what your sexual desires are and what more I can do to please you.
6. Don't be so rejecting of my mother.
7. Let's go out more. You find the baby-sitters sometime.

8. Be more affectionate without sex.
9. Don't take out your hidden resentments against our son.
10. Don't embarrass me with your outspokenness in social situations.
11. Let's do more together, such as go to church, and enjoy it.
12. Give more of yourself when you come home from work.
13. Stop drumming your fingers all the time.
14. Enjoy my music or tolerate it.
15. If you don't want sex, don't give it and then blame me later.
16. Stop biting your nails.
17. Take better care of our things.
18. Tolerate my work and appreciate the life-style it gives us.
19. Be more organized and punctual.
20. Stop turning my statements around.

There you have a considerable list of examples of how people have complained about the behavior of their mate. When I was able to get these objections removed or reduced, the feeling of love toward the other party practically always increased. This should come as no surprise, since it follows Rule No. 1: If somebody does something nice to you, do something nice in return.

SPECIAL TECHNIQUES YOU CAN USE TO EARN MORE LOVE

In addition to the highly rewarding behaviors pointed out previously, ones that are likely to bring out feelings of love, let us focus on some important techniques usually regarded as love-producing actions.

*Determine Your Lover's Physical and Emotional
Tolerance for Intimacy*

I once had a very charming couple to dinner at my
home, and when the woman said good-by she had her
face so close to mine that I was immediately uncomfortable. There was nothing sexual in her act; that was simply the way she began or ended visits with practically
anyone. She liked being up close. If two people happen
to enjoy the same intensity of intimacy, they have a great
advantage over those who have to work this out by trial
and error.

Some couples present this dilemma quite clearly. One
man does not like to sit next to his wife, nor does he enjoy
holding her hand in public, and he does not like to show
affection even if he sits next to her on the couch. Yet he
loves her deeply, treats her very fairly and lovingly, and
is in every other respect a mature and decent human
being.

His wife, on the other hand, complains bitterly that she
does not get enough affection and touching, petting, hugging, or kissing from him. She wants a great deal more
intimacy than he tends to give. It would make her happy
if he would pat her, rub her, hug her, or squeeze her every
time he walked by her. She would think that she was
getting a massage standing up and she would love it. Since
she gets nothing of the sort, the woman is quite unhappy
and does not know what to do. The answer, of course, is
that if he cares for her, he is going to have to make more
of an effort to overcome his physical aloofness and get in
there and make the physical contact. She wants touching
and nothing short of that will do.

Or perhaps she can convince herself that it isn't so necessary after all to be as intimate as she likes and that he
offers so much else in the marriage that there is no need
to make a fuss over this one neglected area. One or the

other of these plans will have to work if the marriage is to succeed. To ignore this vital issue is to invite serious frustration and unhappiness.

Remember that the Words You Use Are Important

What people say and how they say it is not the most important thing in the world. To me, what people do is a great deal more important than what they say they will do. Nevertheless, when we think of the best ways to achieve love, we must recognize that words *are* significant. It happens that, in some of our dealings with each other, what we say and the way we say it is enormously important and has a great deal to do with whether we earn the love of others.

Some people find it very difficult to say, "I love you." Yet there is something almost mystical and almost magical about that phrase. When people hear those "three little words" said with sincerity, they have a feeling of reassurance, warmth, and goodwill that is seldom achieved in any other way. I have interviewed many people who actually think that they must hear the words spoken once in a while if they are to believe that their lovers are devoted to them. In the minds of most individuals it is not enough to be treated in every loving way possible unless the words are spoken also. Women in particular seem to make a greater issue of this than men. This usually causes bewilderment and irritation on the part of men, who insist that they have already shown their love in dozens of ways. Therefore they say: "Why do I have to keep telling her I love her?" These men point out that they are decent husbands who come home on time, do not drink excessively, turn over their paychecks to their wives, and do not raise a fuss if the women want to get together on a Saturday night. As one man put it, "What more could a woman want than a husband who treats her so?"

One could hardly accuse him of being an unloving person when he is indeed kind and generous. Still, his wife will make the point that it is not enough to be treated in a loving way. Love is so much more complete when the words "I love you" are also used.

Those who want verbal reassurances certainly do not have strange desires. Consider: If you have worked very hard at your job and your employers give you a raise, that would show that they appreciated you. But no one *told* you so. Likewise, if you want to show your appreciation to someone, to be completely convincing it is important that you do two things: first, *behave* appreciatively and lovingly toward those whom you want to reward; and second, *tell* them, in actual words, what you feel. The man who was elected president of his soccer club was deeply touched only *after* his friend lavished compliments on him for the new team spirit that was created as a result of the new president's efforts. Being elected president wasn't quite enough. Words of praise also were desired.

Nasty and vulgar words have as much impact in a negative direction as kind and gentle words have in a positive way. If you want to love and be loved, you had better avoid harsh obscenities, put-downs, yelling. Think particularly about yelling.

A yelling man or woman can be likened to a snarling dog, a growling wolf, or a roaring lion. Yelling suggests to the listener that the degree of displeasure, irritation, and annoyance is reaching the point of danger. Why is it that all who listen to yelling are aware of this danger but the ones doing the yelling are not? I have seen any number of men and women in my office who were literally amazed at how far their partners were willing to go to escape them and their yelling. Men in particular do not understand how their wives or their children can take snarling as a very threatening sign. They do not seem to understand how others can become so frightened that they lose their self-assurance and become anxious, worried, or even panicky.

I remember very well the surprise of a man who had been reared in a family where yelling was the usual form of communication. He was never frightened by this. It was just a normal way of speaking. His new bride, however, was raised in a family where never a harsh word was used. She had never been in a quarrel with her parents in her entire life, and you can well imagine what a shock it was when he expressed his annoyances in the loudest tones he could muster and used some of the meanest language he could throw at her. The effect was devastating. She sued for divorce after several of these encounters and was literally physically fearful anytime she was in a room alone with him. It was sad to see how thoroughly amazed the husband was at being rejected and regarded as a dangerous beast. He wept, scratched his head, and exclaimed over and over how what was happening to him was absolutely ridiculous and unbelievable because he was basically a very loving and tender man.

So much for men. Now let's talk about women and their nagging. I fully appreciate the fact that some women do not have the strength to demand their way with men and therefore use gentler and less violent means. Women often have verbal skills superior to those of men; and I can't blame them for resorting to nagging to get their way. What else can they do that is equally effective?

Used with reason and rationed with wisdom, nagging can act like the work of a good fairy godmother prodding us always on to proper action. But overdone—ah, that's another story. Some wives can tell you how they unwisely kept pressing their concerns with endless and unceasing nagging until the patience of their husbands was completely exhausted. Then they found themselves pushed against the wall, heels six inches off the floor, their husband's left hand around their neck, his right fist cocked, ready to shut them up forever.

If you are guilty of this behavior, read on. This book is for you, especially the next two chapters. There you will find the psychological techniques that will permit you to get your way more consistently and with less effort, and often to earn more love than you would otherwise acquire.

Don't Overlove

It may appear strange in a chapter on the best ways to achieve love that I now recommend the keeping of one's kind behavior in check. Strange as it may seem, there is ample evidence in the experience and practice of established therapists to indicate that being too good is not good.

A middle-aged divorced woman did a very creditable job of raising her three children until her husband divorced her. The children were all of such an age that they could choose with whom they wanted to live; and, much to her surprise, they all opted to live with their father. My client was actually a very devoted mother, very responsible, totally concerned with the welfare of her children, and could not understand how they could turn her down when a choice had to be made between her, the loving mother, and him, the normally disciplining father. What hurt even more was the degree of detachment she experienced when she moved a few streets away and realized that her children would not call her up frequently, would not stop by to visit her, and in effect treated her as though she lived two hundred miles away. She could never claim that they were hostile toward her or did not love her. It was simply that they showed no sense of appreciation for what she had done for them, and they repeatedly treated her in a rather matter-of-fact way. That hurt the most.

I have for some years corresponded with a woman in Europe whose story is very similar to the one just cited. She has been totally rejected by her daughter and her son-in-law and the children from that marriage. Yet she insists to me that she has never been mean to any of them, and wanted very much to have their love. She has repeatedly gone out of her way to help these people and to show her love and concern. Nothing seems to make them want to reciprocate.

I find this phenomenon rather fascinating. What I have discovered is that one can normally not love another adult unless one is somewhat fearful of that person as well. This observation does not hold true for helpless beings such as infant children, animals, or elderly and handicapped people. Those latter relationships do not involve giving with the anticipation of future receiving. Adult relationships, however, tend to be much more conditional and require reciprocity for efforts that have been made on behalf of others.

When you love children or adults who are capable of returning your favors (but you do not require them to do so), it is my contention that they will like you but not love you. Those who perform services for which no return is expected (except perhaps money) are not people whom we usually love. These individuals become employees of ours; and although we may appreciate their loyalty, once they leave us we can accept their departure with little regret. We often feel no need to demonstrate further caring for them because they have been paid off.

To create a *mutual* experience of love between two people requires that the deep desires and needs of *both* people be satisfied. When only one party is rewarded, that party is the master and the other is a servant. I concluded that my client, and anyone who is continually giving without receiving, is a servant.

And just how could my client have received reciprocal love from her children? I believe she overloved them when they neglected her. She failed to withhold her services until she was reimbursed, so to speak, with similar services from them. The withholding of affection, services, or favors can start out gently but must always have the potential of making the other person uncomfortable for being neglectful. This is where you get your power to influence the relationship on your behalf. It is when you begin to withhold your *total* acceptance, and make getting along with you a *conditional* thing, that you demonstrate your capacity to create concern, frustration, or even fear in your lover. You are saying by these frustrating acts that you will not tolerate shabby behavior, that you expect a reasonable amount of consideration from your lover, and that if this is not forthcoming, you are perfectly prepared to reject that person in major ways, or completely.

Once your partner or children understand that you have the power to make them feel discomfort and regret over their neglecting you, they are likely to become aware of what it is that you want and what it is that they had better do in order to get you away from your nasty attitude. In short, they will learn that unless they begin to satisfy some of your deep desires and needs, you will make their lives uncomfortable.

Can you now see why a person who is totally giving and who expects nothing in return for his or her services is often not a truly loved person? Total acceptance breeds that kind of one-sidedness. Conditional acceptance, on the other hand, practically forces the other party to consider you and to make your relationship a give-and-take process in which much more is involved than a few simple services or the exchange of money.

All of us have observed that the people who seem to be respected most are those who put up with nonsense least. On the other hand, those who are very yielding, submissive, and humble are often trod upon and easily taken advantage of by people who pounce at the chance of getting as much out of a relationship as they can.

My recommendation to all you saints is that (with the exception of your relationships with infants, helpless animals, and elderly persons) you make your love conditional. Do not give it away for nothing. In order to love and be loved, learn to make your partner, parents, or children somewhat uncomfortable with you if they neglect you. Do this not only for your sake but also for theirs. I say "their sake" because I consider it unfortunate and wrong to raise children, to live with parents, or to engage in a romance without insisting that others show themselves to be reciprocating and sharing persons.

Stand Up to Mock Protest

There is another complex dynamic between lovers that hinges on too much love. This often affects well-meaning men who erroneously believe that giving their partners everything they want is the royal road to romantic success. The more you please someone in practically every way, the more certain you are to have a warm and secure loving relationship—so the thinking goes. It has been my experience not only that it is healthy to disagree with your partner and say "No" every so often but that women in particular *want* their male companions to reject some of their requests.

To understand your female companion and to get her to love and respect you more, it is important that you appreciate the fact that one of the things she wants in a man is that he be strong, ready to make decisions, and a leader on whom she can rely in a tight spot. She looks for strength in her partner.

If a man shows weakness, it scares his woman companion. Instead of having someone who can defend her against family members, strangers, rude salespersons, and disobedient children, she discovers to her horror that her husband is easygoing, pleasant, and a pushover. A love for him will never last if she loses trust in his ability to protect her. Therefore, when she senses that he has qualities of weakness, she will either *(a)* urge him to be stronger until he backs her up (even if it makes him tense) or *(b)* test him.

A woman will test a man by making herself the guinea pig. She will give him a bad time and become uncooperative, difficult, and sometimes just plain flighty to see what the old boy is going to do about it. If he shrugs his shoulders or slinks away, she discovers what she was afraid of: that her so-called protector has weak knees. What she was hoping for all along was that he would stand up to her, show her that he is strong enough to live without her, and that if she rejects him because he cannot or will not please her in every way imaginable, she can very well pack her bags and leave. That is secretly what she wants him to do, because it will prove to her that this man is not a sissy, he has courage, and even she cannot shake him. Proof that she is not necessary to his existence, that she cannot wrap him around her finger, is precisely what she is hoping to find. Pity the man who wants his partner's love so badly that he gets shaky and gives her everything she wants. Little does he realize that he is losing her respect with every inch that he sinks to his knees.

When he does stand up for himself and refuses to be a marshmallow, the woman often screams her head off. She protests loudly that he is being unreasonable, that she deserves what she asks for, that he doesn't love her, and so forth. And the man, seeing all this storm and fury, may feel that his romance is in danger and decide to give in. This is a mistake. What he interprets as a totally rejecting attitude on the part of the woman is still part of her experiment. She has to see whether or not he can stand the heat. What does it take to get him to give in? Will the arguing and accusations weaken the man? If he stands up to her and does not give in to emotions and protests, he reassures her that he is an adult, a mature and strong human being who is not easily swayed by unreasonable and hysterical arguments.

THREE EXCEPTIONS

I have shown that in order to love and be loved, it is critical that you learn to satisfy your partner's deepest desires and needs. But even before this, it is necessary that you understand *what* those deep desires and needs are. Most of the time this is not a difficult matter and might even be learned over a cup of coffee. But sometimes, unfortunately, what it takes to get a person to love you is totally unsuspected. Men need to learn that when they make advances to women, there are exceptions to expected responses.

We have generally been taught that women can be turned on by flattery, jewelry, flowers, candlelight and wine dinners, and all the lovely courtesies that go into seduction. Seduction is the technique men think of first when attempting to be successful lovers. This approach works quite well, *but* only when the woman is in a fairly receptive mood for being seduced.

What is not so generally understood is the power of nonsexual behavior to accomplish the same end. This should not surprise you if you continually keep in mind my definition of love, namely, that we love those who make us happy. Therefore, if a woman would be made very happy to have the children taken to a movie so she can have an afternoon completely free to take a bubble bath and do her toenails, then this becomes an act of seduction. A man who performs these services for her time and again will generally be highly regarded by her. She will think of him as considerate, tender, and very loving. And when a woman is loved she usually becomes amorous also.

This means that a man doing dishes for his wife, helping vacuum the living room, taking her car to the garage to have the oil changed, doing her grocery shopping, or simply talking to her, is performing *sexual* acts. They lead to the bedroom more quickly than do ugly arguments and complaints about not enough love and sex. The sexiest place in the house is not the bedroom, it is practically anywhere else. And the preparation for a sexual evening had better not begin as the two of you are walking toward the bedroom. It is much more successful if it starts in the morning at breakfast.

A second exception to expected behavior that sometimes baffles men is that women do not necessarily enjoy sexual fondling the way men do. To a woman, if she is not in the mood, this is like mosquitoes bothering her when she is taking a sunbath. To have an adoring husband come up behind her when she is at the stove and put his arms around her from the back and fondle her gently is often more of a pain in the neck than a pleasure to her heart. Women sometimes simply do not want to be bothered with sexual advances. They feel as though they are being mauled when men are always after them.

The third exception that men discover is that no matter what they do with some women, the prior conditioning and sexual programming of the female may have been so distorted that nothing the man does can get her to relax sexually. A woman who has been raped, experienced incest, or been rejected by other lovers, or who suffers from other emotional problems can be enormously difficult to love. It is not necessarily a situation that you have created, and it is not necessarily a situation that you are perpetuating. It is a problem that simply exists, because she had those problems before you met her. And getting her to give them up may be beyond your skills or the patience that is required.

Women who go through sexual traumas can develop problems; some become masochistic, some become promiscuous, and others develop sexual inhibitions. The most typical feminine reaction to cruel male behavior is a loss of trust in men, shown as a fear of intimacy. Unless you have seen or experienced fear of intimacy, it is difficult to appreciate how absolutely cautious women *and* men can be about allowing themselves to become vulnerable again.

Those of you who have partners who fear intimacy had better learn to be extremely patient people. Your sex partners are usually not rejecting you out of spite. They simply have been hurt, and their trust has been so shaken that it simply takes a great deal of time to get over their fear. If you behave in normal haste with such a partner, you are going to lose the goal you so strongly desire. But if you are patient, willing to make progress an inch at a time and then to accept relapses, and if you will do this week after week and month after month, you may find that in time your efforts are handsomely rewarded. Woe to you, however, if you get angry, yell, threaten to leave, or call your frightened partner unflattering names. Those are precisely the techniques that led to the problem in the first place, and they are exactly the techniques that can perpetuate the problem.

SUMMARY

In this chapter we have looked at the enormous powers of reinforcement learning. Of the rules for achieving cooperation, respect, and love, this is the most beautiful, and often the most effective.

Rule No. 1 states: If someone does something nice to you, do something nice in return. I have tried to show the particular behaviors other people prize if you want them to love you, but I have also identified particular behaviors about which you sometimes can do very little, even though you are trying to create reciprocal acts of love. Rule No. 1 does not always work, obviously, and it is important that you accept the fact. If reinforcement were always successful, there would be no need for Rules No. 2 and No. 3.

Remember also that, generally speaking, the more you reinforce behavior, the stronger it gets. When a certain behavior exists, you can make the solid assumption that it exists because it is being reinforced by someone. You may not know who is reinforcing and rewarding certain behaviors, because this is sometimes done in a very subtle manner. Nevertheless, if what you are doing does not create the desired changes of behavior, you had better look more deeply into your own actions or look very closely at the actions of others who unknowingly may be rewarding undesired behavior.

A man who complains about his wife's untidy housekeeping practices *but lets her continue* after she has raised her voice, because he does not want to fight, has actually rewarded her for raising her voice. Yet he would say he hates her sloppy housekeeping and her yelling. But he is indirectly responsible for both conditions. This is again proof of the first rule that people will do what they are rewarded for doing. In this case, unfortunately, the behavior that was being rewarded was strongly objected to by the husband but was also being rewarded.

To respond to goodness with goodness requires more courage than is generally realized. Many of us are afraid to be tender, close, open, generous, and friendly—so powerful is the fear of rejection. In the next chapter I will give you a short course in the psychology of fear. Study it well, for the fullfillment of Rule No. 1 is all but impossible unless you are fearless.

Also study very carefully the psychology of anger, or Rule No. 2 will not work. Rule No. 3 requires an understanding not only of fear and anger but also of guilt and other-pity—all four of the emotions that impede the expression of love.

4
The Other Cheek

Rule No. 2 for achieving cooperation, respect, and love is this: If others treat you badly, treat them nicely for a *reasonable* period of time.

You may perhaps notice that the above statement reflects, in part, the message of Christianity. It suggests that when people treat us badly we must first be patient with them, love them despite their sins, turn the other cheek, go the extra mile, sit down and reason with them, and give them time to make changes. This is a beautiful message and implicitly always gives our frustrators the benefit of the doubt. In utilizing Rule No. 2 we assume that we have been wronged, trespassed against, and frustrated: not out of vindictiveness, not out of evil or hostility, but out of misunderstanding and ignorance. That is why we do not immediately want to attack, reject, or treat others disrespectfully when they have behaved in an unacceptable way. We make the assumption that an explanation can get them to understand us better. We hope that if we are patient, the frustrator's behavior will change through enlightenment. We **have** a right to expect that if we treat such people nicely they will lose their defensiveness and appreciate our sacrifice and return our loving act with their own loving behavior. Literature is replete with examples of negative behavior being turned into positive behavior by the bigheartedness of the person who actually did the suffering.

To achieve this degree of patience and understanding, and to be able to control our own natural neurotic and destructive emotions when we are wronged, is not an easy task. Loving your enemies or accepting the sinner, even though you reject the sinning, are skills that can be learned through a great deal of hard work.

In the final analysis we are unforgiving and impatient human beings when we are disturbed emotionally. Those who are impulsive, panicky, jealous, or poorly self-disciplined have the greatest need for serenity when under attack. The more stable you are, the more loving you can be when those around you are unstable. One of the quickest ways in the world to create more neurotic behavior and more injustice is to get just as upset as the one who is doing you wrong. There is very little likelihood of your being an accepting and patient person who can let another person grow (despite an unacceptable experience) if you yourself are hostile, bitter, and hysterical. You will not get good results from treating nicely those who treat you badly unless you learn to control your emotions. In this chapter, therefore, I offer a short course in psychopathology and suggest what you should know about the way emotional disturbances are created and how to overcome them. For fuller expositions of this material I refer you to some of my other books, listed among the Recommended Readings at the end of this volume, which offer help for overcoming various problems. Their subjects include assertiveness— *How to Stand Up for Yourself;* marriage—*Marriage Is a Loving Business; How to Live with a Neurotic;* and self-discipline—*How to Do What You Want to Do.*

THE FOUR OPTIONS

Before going into an actual description of how we create our emotional problems and what we can do about them, or how these emotions interfere with our achieving respect and love, I want you to appreciate why neurotic behavior is so damaging. There are four choices you have in dealing with very frustrating situations. Neurotic behavior is the last of those choices, and it is the one option I do not recommend. You have three other, better options:

Option No. 1: Toleration Without Resentment

The first avenue of approach we often take in dealing with people's difficult behavior is that of toleration without resentment. We tend not to want to make too much of behavior we do not like; we accept it gracefully; we tend to minimize its seriousness; and we convince ourselves, if possible, that it is not a big issue and that we might just as well keep our mouths shut.

We do this many times in our lives, and I think it is wise that we do so. Many of the frustrations we encounter from day to day are hardly worth starting World War III about, and therefore we might as well ignore minor irritations and simply tell ourselves, "That's life." Whenever you do this, you immediately end the frustration, because you are convincing yourself that there isn't any frustration worth being upset over. If not used to excess, this is an extremely mature approach to interpersonal difficulties, and it often shows you off as the more grown-up of the individuals involved. You are someone who has the patience and tolerance not to permit yourself to be unduly frustrated over minor issues.

Option No. 2: Protest

If tolerating things without resentment begins to become more difficult because the frustrations never seem to end, you may want to stop being endlessly patient. Now you do not turn the other cheek, but do the opposite. You protest, make the other person uncomfortable, and become so difficult that he or she begins to see how serious the issue is and how the behavior is going to have to change because you are so annoyed. In using this strategy you go *on strike* or declare a *cold war* until you get what you want.

If this approach does not achieve its purpose and you find yourself becoming very unhappy because of the great tension produced by this cold war, you still have the choice of going back to your first option. You can lump this situation gracefully and without resentment toward those really not worthy of your distress, or you can go on to your next option.

Option No. 3: Separation or Divorce

You don't have to stay with most situations if you don't want to. Fortunately, we usually have a choice of staying or not staying with a job, keeping or not keeping a friend, or preserving or not continuing a marriage.

Separation and divorce now are recognized as proper and fortunate options all of us have at our disposal. When one can no longer tolerate inappropriate behavior, and when it does no good to fight for one's rights because of a partner's resistance, then what other option does a sane person have? The only thing to do then is to leave the unhealthy relationship if one can possibly do so.

Option No. 4: Toleration with Resentment

Possibly the method most often used by many of us in dealing with negative behaviors is simply to get disturbed openly or to let our feelings stew inside and cause physical symptoms. When we tolerate situations or behaviors but deeply resent them, we are laying the groundwork for psychosomatic complaints of all kinds. This is the way we get headaches, stomachaches, colon problems, sleep disturbances, and nervousness. This is how we become depressed or angry, lose interest in life, or develop excessive passivity. We may begin to drink too much and eat too much, or we may not eat enough. Perhaps we begin to have sexual fantasies or actually become unfaithful. And maybe we only bite our nails and cry a little. In any event, the more we tolerate frustrations but continue to resent them, the more we are inclined to be disturbed. This is not a good way to cope with inappropriate behavior. It is in fact the only option of the four which I strongly recommend that you *never* use.

The first three options, though they may cause difficulty for a time, offer hope of eventual relief. By tolerating something without resentment (Option No. 1), we in fact end the pain almost instantly. By protesting and making our partner uncomfortable until he or she changes (Option No. 2), we may go through hell for a while; but most of the time this too brings an end to our suffering. And the same may be said for a separation or divorce (Option No. 3). At first this third option can be very disruptive and painful, but eventually we pick up the pieces of our lives and very often have a better relationship than we had before. It is toleration with resentment (Option No. 4), however, that offers no relief to us. To become resentful and develop all kinds of bad symptoms simply makes our condition worse than it ever was before.

We need, therefore, to learn how not to develop these emotional problems. This is important for two reasons. In the first place, it is painful to be neurotic. Whenever you are upset you are usually hurting yourself more than anyone else. Secondly, it is hard to be a mature person and to offer loving and kind behavior in return for rude and inconsiderate behavior if you are very disturbed. We want to have mature control over ourselves if we are to follow the noble guidance of Rule No. 2 (Turn the other cheek, love your enemies, and go the extra mile). Disturbed people cannot do that. But people who have fine emotional control do it often and do it more easily.

In the rest of this chapter let us consider further two of the options for dealing with frustrating situations: Option No. 1 (Toleration without resentment) and Option No. 4 (Toleration with resentment). We need to learn how to achieve the first kind of toleration. This is essentially what it means in practical terms to "turn the other cheek" as a method to achieve love.

HOW WE UPSET OURSELVES

The most impressive explanation of emotional disturbances to be advanced in many decades is the ABC theory of emotions. Dr. Albert Ellis of the Institute for Rational Living in New York first wrote about this approach over thirty years ago and his views are now gaining international acceptance.

Dr. Ellis states simply that an *activating event* (A) can hurt us only if it is physical in nature. An injury, a disease, a severe temperature change, or the like can only cause us physical harm, not psychological or emotional harm. The *consequences* (C), the pain from the accident, or cancer, or frostbite, for example, are the direct result of A, the physical event. These are facts beyond dispute.

Psychological pain, however, comes not from A, the event, but from the step between A and C, between event and consequences. That step consists of the *beliefs* (B) we have about the event. If we have *rational beliefs* (rB) about the painful events in our lives, we remain largely undisturbed. If we have *irrational beliefs* (iB) about the things that happen to us, we practically always get upset —depending on the degree to which we adhere to the irrational philosophies.

This means that it is *we* who upset ourselves, not other persons or events. Other people do not depress us, or anger us, or scare us. Our irrational beliefs do that.

Simply put, there are twelve irrational ideas that cause practically all of our normal emotional disturbances. Depression is caused by one set of two or three such thoughts. Anger is created when we maintain several other irrational thoughts; and fear, worry, jealousy, procrastination, and passivity also derive from sets of irrational thoughts. If you are ever disturbed, it is important that you try to detect how you are talking to yourself *about* your problems, then decide which of the thoughts that you have are reasonable and which are not. Finally, talk yourself out of believing the foolish and irrational ideas. This, in addition to leading you to practice new behavior, will make you feel differently and cause you to be undisturbed.

For example, not long ago one of my clients told me how very nervous and depressed she became when she realized that she was late to a dinner engagement and that the hostess would be very annoyed with her. I tried to show her that her fear and her depression were not caused because she had forgotten the dinner appointment. Rather, it was what she was saying to herself *about* the fact that she had forgotten the appointment and about how the hostess would feel toward her that caused her to be upset.

I asked her to think for a moment how she reacted when she realized that she was late for the dinner; she immediately said she felt guilty. This woman had upset herself needlessly; did it all by herself, all in her head. Forgetting the dinner or having the hostess angry with her were only *indirectly* related to her being upset.

The way she talked to herself about these two problems caused her depression and her fear. First, she said that she forgot the appointment. That statement is true and therefore not irrational. She also said that she caused her hostess to be frustrated and that this was an undesirable thing to do. That is also true and therefore is not irrational. But these statements cannot explain why she was depressed and tearful. My client also was probably telling herself that because she did these things, she is a bad and worthless person. That *is* irrational. There is no evidence that if you forget an appointment you are an evil human being. My client was not guilty of upsetting the hostess, the hostess was guilty of upsetting the hostess. None of us upsets anyone else. We only upset ourselves. If the hostess wants to lose her poise because somebody was acting like an imperfect human being in forgetting a dinner engagement, that's her problem. If she doesn't want to be upset, either she had better not give any more dinner parties or she had better learn to accept human frailties with calmness. To disapprove of her guest's forgetting the dinner invitation is perfectly sensible; to be unhappy about it is perfectly sensible; and to be annoyed about it is perfectly sensible. But to be mightily disturbed, depressed, angry, or paranoid about it is plainly neurotic.

I tried to show my client how she would have to talk herself into not thinking she was ever a bad person, that these things happen to human beings, and that if she would continually challenge and debate her irrational ideas, she was bound to feel better sooner or later. I then further suggested that she should continue to have contact with her friend, invite her back into her home, and try to patch up the relationship. But she should never feel guilty for what she did or worry much about whether that woman was going to reject her. Rejection is not painful; it is only uncomfortable. But my client could not see that. She honestly believed that not having the other woman's approval was a horrible experience, something like being skinned alive, and that she should do everything in her power to make her friend forgive her, love and think decently of her, forever and ever.

THE TWELVE IRRATIONAL IDEAS

There are twelve irrational ideas with which we upset ourselves and which keep us from tolerating frustration without resentment. If you commit these ideas to memory, you can, whenever you are upset, quickly put your finger on one or more ideas that could be causing your painful emotion. A fuller explanation of why these ideas are irrational is given in my book *Brief Counseling with RET.*

Irrational Idea No. 1: It is absolutely necessary that we adults be loved and approved by the important people in our lives if we want to consider ourselves worthwhile.

Irrational Idea No. 2: If we are not outstanding, accomplished, and achieving, we are less worthy than those who are.

Irrational Idea No. 3: People who are bad, wicked, or villainous must be severely blamed and punished for their wickedness.

Irrational Idea No. 4: It is awful and unbearable when things are not the way we would very much like them to be.

Irrational Idea No. 5: Human unhappiness is caused by external circumstances; thus we have little or no ability to control our sorrows and disturbances.

Irrational Idea No. 6: If something is or may be dangerous or fearsome, we should be terribly concerned about it and keep dwelling on the possibility of its occurring.

Irrational Idea No. 7: It is easier to avoid certain of life's difficulties and responsibilities than it is to face them.

Irrational Idea No. 8: It is reasonable and healthy to be dependent upon others who are stronger than we are, and on whom we can rely.

Irrational Idea No. 9: Our past history is an all-important determiner of our present behavior; if something in the past once affected our lives, it will continue to do so indefinitely.

Irrational Idea No. 10: We should become quite upset over other people's problems and disturbances.

Irrational Idea No. 11: There is invariably a right, precise, and perfect solution to human problems, and it is wiser to do nothing until the right answer has been found.

Irrational Idea No. 12: Beliefs held by respected authorities or society must be correct and should not be questioned.

There you have practically all of the major irrational ideas that can lead to emotional problems. These statements, or variations of them, are the ones with which we knowingly feed ourselves whenever we are confronted with a frustrating situation. And the particular irrational idea or ideas that we put together create different emotions, just as the various ingredients a cook uses in the kitchen determine the final outcome of a meal. If you want to be a stable person, learn to question these ideas for their soundness and their logic. I maintain they are all illogical, irrational, foolish, and ultimately self-defeating. These irrational ideas contribute to depression, with its specific causes: self-blame, self-pity, and other-pity; and they contribute also to anger and fear.

DEPRESSION AND ITS CAUSES

Psychological depression comes from three acts: self-blame, self-pity, and other-pity.

Self-Blame

Whenever you put yourself down, hate yourself, think that you are worthless, and feel terribly guilty over some unacceptable act, you tend not only to disapprove of what you have done but also to disapprove of yourself as a total human being. That is what I call self-blame. Self-blame is a double attack, first on our actions, then on ourselves. The irrational idea behind self-blame is: Unless you are without fault, you are worthless.

To overcome guilt, inferiority, and self-blame, it is important to perform two separate mental tasks. The first is to separate your behavior from yourself; the second is to forgive yourself for having done badly.

How can you separate your actions from *you?* In the same way that you often do it for others. You even do it for animals. If your puppy messes up the house, you're inclined to disapprove of that behavior, but you would hardly hate the dog. If a baby knocks over a valuable piece of pottery, you can certainly regret the fact that the vase was broken, but you certainly don't have to conclude that the child was terrible for breaking it.

It is the same when you perform badly. You are certainly much more than a single act. If you don't do well in a particular subject in school, or if you are not nearly as good at some task as some of your friends are, it only means that others are better students than you are, or that your friends are better car mechanics or perhaps better cooks. Why should being a better student or mechanic or cook make a person better than someone who is not as good at those things? I don't sing well, but the fact that Caruso was a great singer hardly means he was better than I am. I and my behavior are different. I have areas in which I excel, but even if I didn't, there is no logical way I could conclude that I am worthless or bad because I lack certain skills. It is enough to say that I am a poor cabinet-maker without illogically concluding that this makes me worthless as a human being.

Your second important task is to forgive yourself for what you have done, even if you are not hating yourself for a hateful act. Your erroneous behavior arises because you are *deficient, ignorant,* or *disturbed.* For example, you might not have the speed or coordination to be a boxer or a tennis player. Or you may never have been taught these skills. Or you may be so upset that you cannot possibly perform well.

If you are able to conquer self-blame, you will find that it will be a great deal easier for you to tolerate other people's behavior without resentment. You can ask yourself what your mate's problem is and why he or she behaved badly. Was your partner deficient, ignorant, or disturbed? How is it possible to be bitter and resentful toward anyone if you forgive yourself and others?

People who feel guilty are thereby hampered from being loving. In the following pages I will be explaining the strong connection between assertion and love. Excessive passivity is the opposite of assertion and leads to being dominated, not loved. To be assertive requires that you make others uncomfortable. Feeling guilty or sorry for the person you are frustrating makes you weak, dominated, and resentful—not loving. Those two emotions, guilt and other-pity, make self-assertion practically impossible.

From my previous remarks I hope you will have learned not to blame youself when your actions have indirectly upset others. Remember, always, they upset *themselves* about your lack of cooperation. *They* are guilty for being upset. Don't blame yourself for something you could not do even if you wanted to.

Self-Pity

The second major way in which we depress ourselves is by self-pity. It is caused by Irrational Idea No. 4: It is awful and unbearable when things are not the way we would very much like them to be. This world we inhabit is seldom the hospitable and wonderful paradise we dream of. It is sometimes cruel, often vicious, and even more frequently totally unjust. The criminal can literally get away with murder while the desperate and hungry man is sent to prison for stealing just enough food to keep himself alive.

The moment you pity yourself more than just a little bit, try to appreciate the fact that you have just then enormously worsened your life. Not only are you now having to put up with an unfair world but you must now tolerate and suffer the pain of the depression that comes from self-pity. Did you not have enough misery before? Was it not bad enough that your loved one died, or that you lost your job, or that you were perhaps injured? Are not these events sad enough in their own right, so that you would not want another iota of pain added to what you have already been handed by this cruel world? Must you make things worse by getting yourself to the point that you are so low in spirit that you could kill yourself?

Self-pity is fruitless. It incapacitates you. It drains you of the energy to challenge the injustices of this world. And it gets people to leave you alone so that you can nurse your miseries by yourself.

We become self-pitiers by thinking that everything we want we must have, that frustration is terrible and awful, and that life is unbearable because of this unjustice. Fight such a notion. Debate it with yourself and challenge it until you no longer believe that you must have everything you want and that you must be upset just because the world is unfair. Who said it had to be fair? An imperfect world run by imperfect people is not now, never has been, and never will be complete with perfect solutions for all of us. When we get justice, let us consider ourselves lucky.

One of the by-products of self-pity is that those with whom we live become impatient with us. No one likes a crybaby, a whiner, or a complainer. It is far better to work diligently, even feverishly, to change these unkind events if we possibly can, or to accept them with resignation if we cannot. The person who shows the maturity not to collapse in a flood of tears, or to become hysterical, or to be seriously depressed, as though that were going to accomplish a positive end, will earn love and respect. By conquering self-pity we are in an excellent position to face our frustrations and, in facing them, to practice Option No. 1: toleration without resentment.

Other-Pity

The irrational idea that leads us to the sad emotion of other-pity is this: "We should be upset and disturbed over other people's problems and disturbances."

Why should we? What conceivable good do we do for others when we allow ourselves to become upset because of their misfortunes? Does it help them? How? Does it give them courage to go on, or does it rob them of the sense of confidence and the courage to overcome adversity?

Caring and being concerned about someone else's plight is a healthy and ethical stance to take when others are in trouble. We can offer them our assistance, help them to get back on their feet, and be our brother's keeper as we are urged to do by our religious teachings. However, when we become *overcaring* and *overconcerned,* and when we feel *too much* for the suffering of others, we often don't do everything we can for them because we are joining them in their misery. Perhaps misery loves company, but more misery certainly doesn't do much to solve problems.

One of the major faults of overconcern for people's problems is that this indirectly creates neurotic behavior and makes it more difficult for them to cope with the injustices of life. If we do what we can to assist them without feeling sorry for them, while at the same time showing that we care and are concerned, then we are helping them greatly. And by not feeding their sense of self-pity we may help them learn to cope with life.

ANGER

Anger is another of the common emotional problems that troubles practically everyone. Anger arises essentially because we say to ourselves the same thing that the self-pitier does: "It is terrible and awful when I do not get everything I want." But another irrational thought is added: "People are bad and wicked and should be severely blamed and punished for frustrating me." This combination leads to bitterness, resentment, hatred, aggression, and, of course, anger.

Anger is always caused by ourselves, not by someone else, just as psychological depression is caused by ourselves, never by others. The angry person unfortunately believes that if you are a decent and fair person, the things you would *like* to have are things you *must* have. The angry person's *preferences, desires,* and *wishes* become his or her *needs, necessities,* and *demands.* When you convert your wishes to demands and you are not given what you demand, you will suffer the consequences of anger. If you had kept your wishes at the level of the wish and then been frustrated, you would simply have been disappointed or regretful. No one ever gets mad because he or she did not get what was wished for. Ask yourself how many wishes you have had in your lifetime and how many of them have never been satisfied. And how many times did you get angry over the fact that you did not discover a million dollars in your backyard? Or that you were not made a movie star last week? Or that you are not famous? These are all wishes; there are thousands of them, but we are never truly angry when they are not satisfied. When however, even for an instant, we insist that we *should* have our wishes fulfilled, and think that because we are right we must have our way, we then have made a *neurotic demand* out of a *healthy* wish and we suffer a neurotic emotion.

If you never wanted to get angry again in your whole life, it would be theoretically possible to achieve this goal simply by never making another demand out of any of your wishes.

There are two exceptions to the rule that anger is always neurotic. The first is when your anger frightens someone away from a dangerous situation so quickly that an accident is averted. (Yelling at a child might prevent the child's being run over.) The second is when you feel so furious about something that you fight to protect your very life, as when you fight off hoodlums who are trying to rob you. Who cares whether or not your behavior is called neurotic if your strategies have saved either someone else's life or your own?

If you were able to overcome and control anger, how easy it would be to turn the other cheek. You are able to tolerate a situation without resentment because you are literally not making yourself resentful. You are talking yourself out of it. And those of you who are in the habit of continually talking yourself into resentment remember that anything you can talk yourself into you can also talk yourself out of. It is almost impossible to turn the other cheek, to go the extra mile, and to love your enemy if you are going to hate him for doing you a disservice. Instead, let us calmly react to aggravating behaviors in a mature way, denying that *(a)* we have to have what we want, *(b)* those people who frustrate us are evil, and *(c)* evil people are cured if you throw them into dungeons, beat them mercilessly, call them ugly names, and convince them that they are the scum of the earth. What kind of reaction would you expect from someone who is treated violently? Fear, for one. But also hatred.

Fear

Under the heading of fear I include such emotions as worry, anxiety, nervousness, and panic. These are all forms of fear and vary in degree from the least intense, which is worry, to the most intense, which is panic. Fear and worry are created by two irrational ideas: *(a)* it is terrible and awful if things are not the way one would like them to be, and *(b)* if something is dangerous or fearsome, one should think about it, dwell upon it, and focus upon it endlessly in the belief that otherwise things will get worse.

You who are fearful persons see danger and threat in every situation, even in those that are clearly devoid of any danger. You take every unpleasant experience and immediately convert it mentally into a disturbance. You convert a molehill into a Mt. Everest. You get rejected and you think it is the end of the world. If you don't get a promotion, you think it is a horrible experience. Someone steals your parking place and you think it is a catastrophe.

When you describe events in such extreme terms: horrible, awful, end of the world, unbearable, tragic, and catastrophic, you are setting yourself up for a nervous reaction. How else could you feel? Are you supposed to feel calm and serene when you describe what you are facing in such alarming terms?

Examine issues very carefully to see if the one you are facing is really as bad as you say it is. In the vast majority of cases you will find that you are exaggerating, that you are blowing things way out of proportion. This is an extremely common human tendency and is the cornerstone of all emotional disturbances.

Dr. Ellis' claim may sound like fantasy, but consider it very seriously nevertheless. Would you like to know how never to get upset again for the rest of your life? Then take his advice: Never make a catastrophe out of anything again and you will never be psychologically upset again. I know this is hard to believe, but stop and think a bit about how absolutely sensible and accurate that statement is. For example, if you were to describe a rejection as a regrettable event rather than as a horrible one, wouldn't you feel differently? Or if you thought of a demotion as a sad event rather than as a tragic one, wouldn't that make a difference to you? In other words, if you define or describe what happens to you in less alarming terms, such as regrettable, unfortunate, disappointing, sad, annoying, or irritating, you would feel simply *normally* frustrated. But when you describe them in drastic ways, you are not only going to be frustrated, you are going to be frightened, scared, nervous, and worried out of your skin.

Try to imagine how difficult it is for you to be calm and resigned to unfortunate events in your life (Rule No. 2) if you think that every bad event that happens to you is the end of the world. How can you tolerate something without being mightily upset if everything you don't like is a calamity? There is no way you can keep your stability and maturity and continue to carry on a pleasant relationship with someone if you are going to allow yourself to be destroyed emotionally because your perception of the entire event is way out of proportion. That is why the control of your fear is among the most important psychological tasks you need to learn.

Excessive passivity is unfortunately one of the forms of fear that destroys a great deal of happiness in very gentle people. If you are one of those who hate to assert themselves, you are among the unhappiest of all the persons I encounter. Yet it is a pity that there are not more beautiful and giving people such as you. You do need to learn, however, not to be a coward when the need arises to stand up for yourself. I find there are five reasons why we act as cowards. Two of them are environmental and three are psychological.

The first reason why we behave as cowards is that we are afraid of being hurt physically. This makes good sense when you are facing a gorilla. If you know you are going to be pounded into the ground, run for your life. Nobody in his right mind wants to take on a physically superior opponent if he or she knows there is no chance of winning.

The second reason why we behave as cowards is that we are afraid of financial loss. The boss is always right. He writes out the checks, and it is his business. If you don't like what he is asking you to do, quit. If you value your job, don't argue with him too strenuously or you will find yourself out on the street.

The third reason why we are timid and back off from our own convictions is that sometimes we are not sure of ourselves. We think, "Wouldn't it be awful if I made a mistake?" Suppose you wanted to buy a house but your mate argues strongly against it. Since you can't know with certainty who is right, and because you have a great fear of being wrong, you give in to your lover's decision. In the end you wind up very seldom getting things to go your way. What is so wrong about being wrong? If you make a decision and it turns out to be an unwise one, so be it. One of the best ways to learn how to make sound decisions is to make many decisions. The more experience you get, the more you are going to learn what to consider in making smart decisions. If you don't take the opportunity to learn by your errors, your partner does.

The fourth reason why we don't stand up for ourselves is a fear of injuring the other person's feelings. After all, not giving people what they want often leaves them angry, depressed, hurt, resentful, and tearful. What you need to understand, however, is that you have not hurt that person's feelings. You can only hurt people physically, not emotionally. If someone wants to get depressed, angry, or nervous over one of your acts, that's *their problem,* not yours. They take that frustration and insist upon *converting* it into an emotional disturbance. Then they have the gall to turn around and say to you, "Look how you are upsetting me." Your response should be: "Oh, I'm sorry, dear, but you are doing this to yourself. Why don't you read a book, or go talk to a clinical psychologist about your disturbance? I certainly don't want to see you disturbed every time I make a suggestion that you don't like. I hope you get over your problem very soon."

And the fifth general reason why we do not assert ourselves is that we fear rejection. We think rejection is painful, that it *has* to hurt, and that not being loved or approved by others is among the most horrible experiences in the whole world. Certainly being rejected hurts, but no more than we allow it to. You have probably had the experience of being upset by the rejection of people whom you eventually didn't really much care about. At first rejection hurt, then you didn't care at all. Why is that? Because you convinced yourself that you didn't need that person's love and approval. Suppose you could have told yourself that immediately upon the first rejection? Can't you see how you would have been spared a lot of unnecessary pain?

The next time you are rejected, simply convince yourself that you do not *need* the love of other people, even if they are your mates, your children, or your parents. This does not mean that I think love is unimportant. Far from it. I regard it as a very important element in life. I think it is something we want to strive very hard to maintain at all times. However, if for a period of time, with a particular person, you are not having the kind of loving relationship that you want, it is hardly a catastrophe. It is not tragic; it is just regrettable. Do what you can to improve the situation and if it doesn't work, don't worry. There are always other people that one can love. As long as you have someone who will rent you a room and sell you gasoline and food, you have people who like you. That's important, and it's equally important to make sure people don't hate you. Those who can stab you in the back are much more a cause of concern than someone who doesn't love you. So if you want to be greatly concerned about anything, be concerned about being hated, not unloved.

I have reviewed only briefly the self-defeating emotions that make it very difficult to achieve toleration without resentment (Option No. 1). Suppose you want to be a mature and loving person despite the negative behavior of another. You cannot achieve this goal if you are highly disturbed. To return goodness for evil you are required to be in control of yourself.

THE WEAKEST LINK:
RATIONAL SELF-DEBATE

One of the major contributions made by Rational-Emotive therapists is their great emphasis on self-debate as an excellent method for overcoming emotional disturbances. The ABC theory of emotions (explained earlier in this chapter) can help us locate the irrational beliefs causing our upsets. It is then necessary to go to the next step, that of *disputation* (D), or rational self-debate.

In order to change your attitudes it is necessary to give more than just lip service to the need for change. It is essential that you examine your belief system so thoroughly that you are totally convinced that what you have been taught all your life is probably incorrect and that these new rational views are much more sane. To do that, however, it is critical in dealing with frustrations that you do a great deal of challenging, debating, and analyzing of your self-talk. You can make the assumption that if you are still upset, you have not talked yourself out of your irrational nonsense. The only way you will know whether your debating over irrational ideas is working a change is when you feel relieved of the painful emotions that came from the irrational beliefs. If you *are* guilty for upsetting someone and you start believing the idea that you are responsible for what they are going through, and you find that you are still *feeling* guilty, you have to conclude that you have not debated hard enough. Get back on target. Debate again the false notions that you can literally upset people by your actions, that they have no responsibility for their emotions, and that it is your responsibility to change so that they will feel less upset. If you are still feeling guilty, you have lost the argument.

The major shortcoming most people have in their effort to become emotionally healthy human beings is that they don't argue with themselves enough. They keep reinforcing neurotic beliefs such as these: they must be perfect, it is terrible if they are not loved, people who behave badly are themselves bad, it is easier to avoid difficult tasks than it is to face them, and so on. Unless you argue with yourself against this nonsense, you are not apt to change. Debate, debate, debate with yourself until you become thoroughly convinced that you do not have to be perfect in order to be acceptable; you do not have to be loved in order to be acceptable. People are allowed to make mistakes and still be acceptable because they are not the same as their behavior, and facing difficult tasks is easier than not facing them.

Assuming you have taken step D, debating vigorously with yourself each time you become upset, you will find two more stages or *effects* (E) occurring before the cycle of correction is complete. The first will be a *cognitive effect* (cE) and the second an emotional or *behavioral effect* (bE).

The cognitive effect comes when your disputing changes your thinking. You begin, in other words, to see the fallacy in your irrational thinking. You can truly see how, for example, rejection is not disastrous unless you think it is, or that not getting what you deserve is not cause for anger.

The behavioral effect comes when you actually feel better. Only then will you be convinced of the soundness of your self-debate. When you feel calm rather than worried, or confident rather than threatened, you will naturally conclude that you have gone through the ABC's as well as the D's and E's of emotional disturbances correctly and have talked yourself back into health and stability.

Study carefully the list of irrational ideas, and if you do not see how irrational they are, read further in my book *Brief Counseling with RET,* or in Ellis and Harper's *A New Guide to Rational Living,* where fuller discussion is given to show that those ideas are truly inaccurate. It is critical that you convince yourself that they are silly and dangerous. Then you will be able to practice Rule No. 2: If someone does something bad to you, do something nice in return, but only for a *reasonable* period of time.

Who Responds to Rule No. 2

There is a beauty and a majesty to returning goodness for evil. It is a noble principle, one that has been prominent in the major beliefs of a number of religions. We have been taught that anyone who is shown enough love and given enough patience will eventually react to our love and change for the better. Love is thus defined as nothing short of an endless giving process. If a sinner has not been changed by whatever we have done so far, we are encouraged to be patient, to pray, to see him or her as a child of God, and to have faith that our good actions will eventually soften those unfeeling attitudes.

The teaching that we should forgive those who trespass against us is so strong that we seldom ask ourselves how

much we are expected to bear before we cease being
tolerant. Unfortunately, people feel that when they forgive someone for an unkind act they are also not supposed
to penalize the person for it either. The teaching that we
should forgive those who trespass against us does not say
anything about not penalizing those who have injured us.
Is it not possible to be completely forgiving and loving of
those who do us wrong and, at the same time, *because* we
want to continue to love them, to correct them for their
wrongdoing? Forgiveness does not require that misbehavior be accepted, only that we not hate the person because
of the unacceptable act. In short, I can forgive my child for
wrecking the car; and even while I take her license away,
I can still be very fond of her and loving to her. Because
I make her pay the damages and I do not let her have
access to the car until she proves to be more responsible
does not indicate that I hate her. Rather, I demonstrate
forgiveness and love on the one hand, and at the same
time I show firmness and willingness to correct her behavior.

Who responds well to the practice of reacting to bad
behavior with loving acts, up to a point (Rule No. 2)? The
answer is fairly obvious. It is the mature, the grown-up, the
stable, and the emotionally untroubled person who benefits by our forgiving and loving behavior. Troubled and
immature people do not benefit from the generosity
shown in Rule No. 2.

A mature person, when it is pointed out to him or her
that some behavior was unfair, readily responds with an
apology and an attempt to make restitution. If a man
tells his wife that she has been tardy a number of times
lately and that he wishes she would change, and if she is
mature and well adjusted, she will readily acknowledge
the fault and reassure him that she is making every effort
to change. Giving her a second, third, or fourth chance
to change makes sense because she knows she has a

problem and obviously needs time to conquer it.

You are wasting your time, however, after it becomes clear that your efforts are not working. When returning good for evil gets you nowhere, and you begin to sense, after several or many more trials, that things are actually getting worse rather than better, the only sensible conclusion you can come to is that you are dealing with a highly troubled or very immature person. It should become obvious to you that communicating at a mature level is not possible. You are talking a language that he or she does not understand. In fact, you have apparently been making matters worse because you have been rewarding poor behavior.

You can tell that your kind behavior is backfiring *(a)* when your partner or child is not changing after a few trials, *(b)* when that person seems not even to care enough to try to change, or *(c)* when the person tells you outright that he or she has no intention of changing. What more do you need to know? Is not the handwriting on the wall? If you need more proof that returning good for bad is not working, then you have more of a problem than the other person does. It should be obvious that Rule No. 2 (return good behavior for bad for a reasonable period of time) is not working if no change actually occurs after a reasonable period of time. At this point you may need to move on to Rule No. 3. To do otherwise is immoral.

5
The Last Resort

What are you supposed to do when things get so bad with your family, friends, or employers that you feel you can no longer tolerate their inconsiderate behavior? Surely anyone would agree that there comes a time when patience runs out and tolerance reaches an end. As wonderful as it would be if we could have infinite patience and continue to love those who trespass against us, that is for most of us more of an ideal than a practical way of life. Only saints and martyrs can put up endlessly with injustices and manipulations. The rest of us are normally self-interested and simply are not able to tolerate rude, inconsiderate, and unjust behavior for more than a reasonable length of time. But what do we do then?

We do what we have always done since the beginning of time. We rebel and fight back. In short, we follow Rule No. 3: If someone does something bad to you, do something bad to him or her (but without anger and, at first, with equal intensity).

JUSTIFICATION FOR RULE NO. 3

If you have been raised to be a peaceful and cooperative individual, you certainly will not take kindly to this last piece of advice. There is something unpleasant and demeaning about the suggestion that we should return bad behavior for bad behavior. I feel as you do that it somehow goes against our higher sensibilities and our wish to be mature. Yet what are you to do when reason does not work, when you have been patient, have gone the extra mile, have turned the other cheek, and have tried to sit down and discuss your mutual difficulties rationally, but nothing works? You would truly be a fool to keep on pursuing a strategy that is blatantly inefficient. Your only recourse is to make your frustrator *uncomfortable* until the offending behavior has ceased or is sufficiently altered.

If a certain amount of discomfort does not bring about the changes that you were looking for, then increase the discomfort. If that does not work, then go even farther and make your opponent even more uncomfortable. How far should you go? As far as is necessary to get the result you are looking for.

Remember the four options for dealing with frustration, given at the beginning of Chapter 4? Option No. 2 (Protest) states that if you find that you cannot tolerate a situation without resentment, you should make a protest, go on strike, or declare a cold war until you get the changes you want. And if that does not work, you can always go back to Option No. 1 (Toleration without resentment). If you can't live with that, you can always go on to Option No. 3 (Separation or divorce). Rule No. 3, which tells us to reward bad treatment with bad treatment, deals with the second and third options. It says that the time for being nice is over and the time for being tough is beginning. When people step on your toes and won't stop doing it, then it's time for you to step on their toes. This downward spiral can continue until so much pressure is built up that someone may give in to preserve the relationship.

I feel that the resistance people will have against employing Rule No. 3 could be so strong in some instances that unless a clear justification is given, it will be difficult for them to adopt it. Interestingly enough, of the three rules I have given (at the end of Chapter 1), only this third rule requires justification. Everyone agrees that if one is treated nicely, it is quite appropriate to respond in an equally nice way (Rule No. 1). And few would quarrel with the idea that if one is treated badly, it is best not to immediately get even (Rule No. 2). However, the advice to get nasty with people who are nasty with us, when other methods have failed (Rule No. 3), is clearly a whole new approach.

Yet, is it new? Although the second rule admonishes us to forgive those who annoy us, don't forget that there is a great deal of similarity between some behavior of our great religious leaders and the third rule. Strange as it may seem to those who do not know the New Testament story, Christ used Rule No. 3. When he disapproved of the mercenary use to which the Temple was being put by money-lenders and merchants, he drove them out. Remember also that the Maccabean leaders of the Jewish people were strong and unyielding. They did not turn the other cheek. When pushed to extremes they fought back, they resisted, they made opposing armies very uncomfortable.

Gandhi did not, in a great gesture of tolerance, allow the British to dominate his nation. He was anything but yielding. Although he was nonviolent, he was nevertheless difficult to deal with, uncooperative, and resistive in all ways. He annoyed the British government with his lack of cooperation for so long and so greatly that eventually India won its independence.

And what about American black leaders in the last thirty years? Martin Luther King used Gandhi's methods with great success in acquiring greater civil liberties for the black people of the United States. His method was nothing short of the use of Rule No. 3. When blacks were fed up with being asked to move to the back of buses, he led them to boycott the buses. There it is. That is the behavior I am advocating; all of us use it when reason does not seem to have any effect on our frustrators.

If I have not convinced you yet that there is a justification for returning bad behavior, and if my reference to religious leaders or civil rights leaders does not move you, then let me take you into the psychological laboratory. Remember how behavior is influenced? If an act is rewarded or reinforced in any way, it becomes stronger. The likelihood of a person, a family, a group, or a corporation behaving in a certain way depends upon whether or not such behavior has previously been rewarded or penalized. When a behavior pattern is not rewarded, it tends to be weakened. From learning theory we also have the concept of extinction, which describes how human behavior can be diminished or stopped.

All of these insights lead us to one conclusion: when behavior continues to exist, it exists because it is rewarded. If we want change and none occurs, we must conclude that the behavior is *still being rewarded.* It may be we or others who are doing the rewarding. It may sometimes be difficult to determine who is reinforcing the behavior and how that is being done. Nevertheless, behavior that continues to exist, exists because it is being reinforced.

It is time we fully appreciated this fact. All the good or bad that comes from humans is *our* responsibility. We are not responsible for earthquakes, storms, or droughts; and trees, rocks, and clouds are not responsible for people's behavior. People are responsible for people's performances.

In greater or lesser degree it is we—you and I—who are responsible for poverty, war, crime, child abuse, and thousands of deaths each year on our highways. Why you and I? Because trees, rocks, clouds, and rabbits don't cause war or divorces. Human behavior is controlled largely by humans.

Therefore, logic clearly tells us if we want a behavior not to continue, we had better stop reinforcing it. The one who is doing the reinforcing must stop that practice. This means further that if we want behavior to change in someone else, *we must change first.* Unless we give these troublemakers a new person to deal with, they will simply feel quite comfortable in dealing with us in the same old way we so detest. In other words, we must stop reinforcing the behavior that we are complaining about. We frequently and unwittingly *make* the problems that we are trying mightily to stop. And closer examination often shows us that *we* are the ones who are creating our own headaches. We are 49 percent responsible for the irritating things people do to us because we tolerate these irritations so easily. The other parties are 51 percent responsible because, in the final analysis, it is they who are behaving unacceptably.

For example, if you are in the habit of giving expensive presents to members of your family for Christmas and on birthdays but they reciprocate only with token gifts or cards, although they are able to do better, then it is quite clear that you have trained them to do that to you. Obviously they don't think there is anything wrong with expecting an expensive gift from you while they can get by with a 50-cent card. If you tolerate such a situation more than a few times, you will *train* them to treat you in the same way in the future.

In order to stop such inconsiderateness you can stop giving them presents on Christmas, birthdays, or Valentine's Day. If that troubles them, they will quickly get the message: if they want nice things from you again, they had better start doing their fair share, reciprocating in a mature and equal manner.

RATIONALIZATIONS FOR BEING PASSIVE

When you have tried your best to be gentle and persuasive in showing others how they are being inconsiderate, and you find that this does not work, it is more difficult than most people realize to go on to follow Rule No. 3 (Reward bad treatment with bad treatment), using the option of protest and strike. No one relishes the prospect of unpleasant confrontations that often can be long and drawn out. Confrontation can start ugly scenes and perhaps even rip a relationship apart. So, rather than take these chances, people will avoid conflict and use a number of rationalizations to justify this avoidance.

The first and most common excuse used by those who will not stand up for themselves is the fear of the fighting and yelling that often ensues when we put pressure on others to change. Nobody likes to change, and the longer people have had their way, the louder they are going to squawk when they are made uncomfortable. Even when men and women are not violent and are not expected to become so, the possibility of their yelling and saying ugly and nasty things strikes fear in the hearts of most people. It seems as though they are about to be attacked with daggers.

I agree that all hell can break loose when you stop being the patsy you once were and you begin making other people somewhat miserable. However, as Dr. Ellis repeatedly points out, it is easier to face difficult problems than it is to avoid them. After months or years of being a sweetheart you may have gained nothing but a whole host of psychological problems. You have lost considerable feeling for your lover. You are daily fantasizing about what it would be like to leave your relationship. You get all these painful consequences by believing that it is easier to give in to a dictator than it is to fight one. This is one of the most frequent excuses my clients give me when I try to get them to see that they can no longer improve their relationships if they continue to turn the other cheek. If they want any change, they had better get tough and stand up to the tyrants in their lives. And the most common response they give is: "But I can't stand a fight. I can't stand the yelling. He will get so mad and yell. She'll get hysterical and take off and leave me."

I agree with you that all of these consequences are possible. What you may not understand, however, is that if you do not stand up for your rights at this point, if you feel that you cannot tolerate the situation without resentment, you do not have any other choice. I recommend that you return negative behavior with negative behavior and teach that other person not to treat you so shabbily. In most instances what results is only a lot of angry talk. In the final analysis this cannot hurt you. Words do not hurt, no matter how nasty they are. A word is a vibration that comes from the other person's throat, passes the lips, sets air waves in motion, goes across the room, and lands on your eardrum. You are bombarded with these kinds of vibrations at all times; and unless they are literally of the intensity of an explosion, they are harmless. It makes no difference whether a person says, "Fool," or "I hate you," or "Witch." These words are all harmless sounds landing on your ear. If you don't agree with those sounds, ignore them. If they happen to be true, acknowledge them and tell your partner that he or she is right and that you will do whatever you can to change, because you don't want to be that way. But in most cases, of course, you will not feel that you are guilty of all the things you are accused of. So why should you be afraid of some noise? At sporting events or in a movie house you hear sounds that are many times louder than those you hear in an argument in your own kitchen.

Now you may complain that it is not the sound of the voice that bothers you but the meaning behind it. You fear that you are going to be rejected, unloved, and deserted. But does that usually happen? How many arguments have you had and the marriage did not dissolve? You will have to agree that it is a rare marriage that falls apart at the end of a single violent argument. In most cases it takes numerous disputes to rip a relationship apart. Therefore, in order to stop these fights, stop tolerating them. If you want the respect, cooperation, and love of your partner and you now realize that being a nice guy or gal has not achieved that end, stop being nice. Get a little tough. Make the other person *somewhat* fearful of you. You'll be amazed at how quickly you may get things turned around.

A second reason why people make excuses for not wanting to move to Rule No. 3 is that they are afraid that when they decide to become uncooperative they will hurt other people's feelings.

In our discussion of Rational-Emotive Therapy, however, we learned that *you* cannot upset other people emotionally. If they want to get upset over your asserting yourself, that is *their* problem. They don't seem to mind doing things *you* don't like, so why should you mind doing things they dislike? Even if your partner becomes depressed, I still insist that this is not something you are doing to anyone. It is what they are doing to themselves. As a matter of fact, when you begin to become somewhat difficult, you can usually expect a series of strategies from the other person to make matters worse and worse. They are done for your benefit, to weaken you and to make you back down.

Suppose a woman is fed up with her husband's coming home late. He refuses to telephone her from the bar where he stops with his buddies, and then comes home at eight or nine and expects her to have a warm supper waiting for him. This has happened a good number of times to women with whom I have counseled. When they are finally so depressed and angry that they want to walk out on the marriage, they come in to see me, ready to hear my advice to tell their husband what they will tolerate and what they won't. I suggest to them that if the husband is not home at the usual time when the family eats, the wife and the children should eat by themselves. After they have eaten she should put all the rest of the food away. Let him make his own supper.

Some men will then begin to employ a series of strategies to make the wife back down. The husband may first yell his head off and try to justify his behavior by claiming that he works hard all day long. He may say that no woman has a right to tell him what to do, that he is never all that late anyway, and that it is her duty to have a warm supper for him when he comes home regardless of what time it is. If she does not give in to the yelling and the fist-shaking, he may then proceed to get nastier by coming home later. Instead of coming home at nine, now he may decide to come home at 1:00 A.M. And if that doesn't work, he will speed up the tempo by threatening to step out on her. Or he may want to "drop the atom bomb" and tell her she had better shape up or he will divorce her.

If you meet each of these storms knowing that you are facing a series of counterattacks, you can simply endure them. Do not become frightened. Be prepared for the worst. But believe in the experience of hundreds of people who have been amazed at how quickly others give in when they realize that none of their threats are going to work.

As a matter of fact, if you launch some handy counterattacks against the first assaults made upon you, you will be showing your partner in no uncertain terms that you are a changed person and are through tolerating the relationship the way it was. If, in the example above, the woman were to stop doing the man's laundry because he was coming home late, she might really shock him. And then if he threatened to have an affair, she could pack up the kids the very next night and stay in a motel for a few days to show him she can get nasty too!

Obviously, none of this is possible if you are always *overly concerned* about the other person's feelings. Once you get over the inaccurate notion that you can hurt someone emotionally, you are capable of decisive actions. But as long as you believe that you are responsible for another person's feelings, you will never take the necessary steps. If you do not act, however, I assure you there will be a cold day in hell before you get that person's cooperation, respect, and love!

WORDS VS. ACTIONS

When your feelings warn you that you are reaching the end of your patience in any relationship, you may wonder why the efforts you have made thus far have not brought relief. One common explanation for this disappointing state of affairs is that you may have assumed that the many discussions, complaints, and loud arguments constituted reasonable efforts on your part. What you may not realize is that talking is a strategy of returning good for evil (Rule No. 2). It directs you to sit down and reason with your friend, employer, parent, child, or lover. You may think you are applying Rule No. 3 when you argue loudly, but it is still one of the strategies of the second rule. *Words* belong to Rule No. 2, *actions* belong to Rule No. 3. It is time that you stop saying what you will do and instead do what you say you will. There is an enormous difference between a word and an action, even though there may be a great deal more heat created with an argument than there is with frustrating counter behavior.

If words and reasoning have not worked, my advice to you is to shut your mouth and *do* something about the situation. I find that people listen much better with their *eyes* than they do with their *ears*. Time after time in my practice I have come across men and women who were shocked into realizing how quickly their relationships were changed by a single dramatic act by one party that instantly made an enormous impression on the other.

When people are sick and tired of complaining, they

tend to take four actions that bring their message home in unmistakable terms. The first is to see a lawyer. The second is to seek out a marriage counselor. The third is to leave home. And the fourth is to have an affair. These powerful actions require no further words to make an issue abundantly clear.

Acting instead of talking seems to be a difficult concept for people to grasp. Even when they finally do act, they think it is necessary to go back to the verbal level again and to explain why they have done what it is they have decided to do. They feel they must *explain* or *apologize* or *warn* over and over again. This is not so; an act is worth a thousand words. It says all that one needs to say, namely, "Change, or the actions will become even more frustrating."

Do not back down once you have launched yourself on the road of protest. You are on strike. You have declared a cold war. The moment things get hot is the time when you will know that you are finally getting through to your frustrator. And you will not let up on this program until you get the results you want. You want to be just reasonably content, and excuses are unacceptable. I caution against listening to excuses such as these: "I can't stop drinking because I have an emotional problem." "I am afraid of sex, and I just can't take the initiative." "I never did like housework. It bores me." "I don't know how to make the children mind." "I can't just leave a bar when the guys have bought me a couple of rounds of beer and I haven't taken my turn to buy them drinks."

The only thing you are interested in is that *behavior must change.* How the excuse makers will solve their problem is up to them. The woman with sex problems had better make a strong effort to overcome them or get professional help. The man who has a drinking problem had better control it through sheer willpower or get the necessary help and learn to control it. We are not greatly interested in how they do it, *only that they do it.*

Other-pity is the great obstacle to the firmness it takes not to back down once you have embarked on a course of action. The moment you begin to feel sorry for the other person is the moment you weaken. Other-pity is the weak link in an otherwise strong chain when parents let a child watch television before he has finished his homework. Tears, arguments, and getting depressed are all common reactions the other person uses to play upon your sympathies. Remind yourself that the problem belongs to the other person and that he or she will only get worse if you don't take a hard-nosed attitude and stop making exceptions. To say, "O.K., John, I'll let it go today, but tomorrow you had better come in on time or I'll have to penalize you," is to make a meaningless threat unless you are really prepared to levy penalties. Actions convince people of what you mean, not words.

A teen-age boy was warned by his parents that he could not under any circumstances drive the car until he had his license. The boy disobeyed twice; and each time he got a sermon that lasted a half hour, warning him of the enormous dangers into which he was putting his family. He was reminded that he could be in serious trouble with the law, his car keys would be taken away for a long time, and if he had an accident his father could be sued and put into financial jeopardy for years.

His parents felt sympathetic for his yearning to get behind the wheel but had the good sense to realize that it was simply dangerous to let him do so until he was legally able. I diagnosed their weak link as other-pity and told them that if they did not sell the car immediately, they would only be teaching the boy that they did not mean what they said. They went home and within a day sold the car without warning. The son was angry, hurt, and shocked at the suddenness of this move. But the severity and swiftness of their action toned him down remarkably well, and he began to show a great deal more respect from that day forward.

Things do not, of course, always work out this smoothly. In another instance, a teen-age girl barged into the home and rudely asked her mother, in front of company, if she could borrow some money. The mother took the girl aside, scolded her, and refused to give her what she wanted. Since then the girl has given her mother the cold shoulder, and this has been going on for months.

The mother felt that she had botched things up because things were now worse than they were before. I disagreed. The rejection she is getting from her daughter is the price she paid for respect. You can't expect to be a top sergeant and at the same time expect to be loved by the people you order around. I advised the mother that she could very nicely do without the daughter's approval since the daughter was apparently perfectly capable of doing without the mother's approval. Secondly, if she were nice to the daughter in every other respect and was courteous, unangry, and as friendly as the girl would allow, it would be very difficult for the child to continue to be angry at the mother forever. The lesson the child was to learn was that if she wanted her mother's cooperation in the future, she would have to stop being rude, selfish, and discourteous. Under no circumstances was the mother to back down on her requirements for decent behavior.

If the mother were to become lenient with this nasty behavior, she would be encouraging the girl to be rude from that day forward.

Can we always take a stand and stick with it? Of course not. Sometimes people have more power over us than we have over them, and at those times it is only sensible that we give in to avoid consequences so serious that no reasonable person would want to encourage them.

I read of such an example when I was in England to promote my books. Bandits threatened to blind an eleven-year-old girl unless her father handed over the keys to his safe. To avoid having them pour caustic cleaning fluid on her, the father paid the bandits the ransom money. Was he reinforcing their criminal behavior? Certainly he was. In this instance he had no choice. The money was of secondary consideration compared to the health of his daughter. He reasoned correctly that perhaps the criminals might be caught at some future date. This is one of those exceptions when other-pity (fear for his daughter's life) was totally justified.

At times people's attempts to protest with *actions* rather than *words* wind up being very inefficient because the actions are more self-damaging than they are damaging to the other party. If you pressure others, you certainly don't want to frustrate yourself too! Deciding to act instead of talk is going to cost you aggravation enough, I can assure you; making things additionally difficult for yourself is simply unwise.

If a wife, to spite her husband because he doesn't care about his health, puts on a great deal of weight, she is obviously putting herself in jeopardy. He may smoke, drink, and never exercise even though he has had heart surgery, and it is just possible that her becoming obese might eventually disgust him enough to change his own habits. But wear and tear on her own body is, in my opinion, too great a price to pay for his faults. When you return nasty behavior for nasty behavior, try to make sure that you are hurting yourself as little as possible in the process. When the husband of one of my clients treated her belongings with disrespect, slammed doors, broke windows, pulled the padding out of chairs, and put holes in the walls, she smashed the culprit's record player. It was an expensive item, and he hasn't broken anything in months. Unfortunately she felt ashamed of what she did, rather than proud. She had sunk to his level and felt she was no better than he. And this brings us to the consideration of a very important issue when we fight fire with fire.

LOWERING OURSELVES TO GET EVEN

If you have the same sensibilities that I have, and I believe most people have, you will no doubt find carrying out Rule No. 3 rather distasteful. Not only are you required to go against your tender nature and no longer care excessively how others feel, but to make this program work most effectively you will have to lower yourself to the level of your opponent. This is not easy for mature people. However, we are dealing with immature and troubled people. We have already learned that our treating them at a higher level only makes them worse. Unfortunately, when we approach them at a more civilized level we are not making ourselves understood. We conclude, therefore, that we must talk their language, and doing things to them similar to what they are doing to us *is* talking their language. That's regrettable, but it is necessary unless you want to tolerate such behavior, or unless you definitely want to leave the relationship. There is no free lunch; and if you want change, you simply have to continue to lower yourself to more and more drastic methods until you get the desired results. Then you will not be faced with the utter frustration of having to say, as one of my clients did, "The only thing I can think of is to talk until I'm blue in the face." That is what we are trying to avoid.

The people around you may be shocked at the change in your behavior, and they may well give in to you more quickly because they may conclude there is no way of changing your craziness. You will have to develop a thick hide to accomplish this, because it is so out of character for you. This can be accomplished by not catastrophizing, not pitying yourself, and not pitying the other person.

Accepting Rule No. 3 does not mean that you will become insulting or angry and thereby show yourself to be thoroughly immature also. You will only be acting in an uncooperative fashion because you are forced to do so for your sake and for the sake of the other person. I specifically want to emphasize this point: Asserting yourself *never* has to be done with hatred or anger. In fact, assertiveness usually will not work if you allow yourself to become highly emotional and physically aggressive. It simply means that you will be difficult to get along with, while at the same time you will be smiling and friendly. You will be detached and not overly concerned about whether you are being loved in the process.

A good example of lowering yourself to the strategies of those who frustrate you would be to refuse to be sexually cooperative. Simply insist there will be no sex until things change to a reasonable degree.

All of us are assertive people, and the only difference between us is *when* we will decide to employ that assertiveness. I believe that we all can become intolerant of aggression if the cause is great enough. For no apparent reason a teen-age girl was singled out in the most rejecting ways at school. The children would move to another table when she sat down at theirs. They would trip her in the hallways. And when she was on the dance floor the boys got great pleasure from turning on her, calling her names, and then walking away. My recommendation was that she not tolerate such abuse and that she fight back. When kicked, she kicked back. When nasty kids sat near her, she moved away; and when she was asked to dance, she refused. She obviously made no friends in that group, but they learned to leave her alone.

Lowering yourself to the level of your attacker is not always going to work, of course, and is not always the preferred way to act. Just think of the Irish insurgents who starved themselves to death, hoping to force the British government to recognize them as soldiers rather than as criminals. Or consider the woman who wanted to divorce her husband because he took drugs, but said: "I vowed to accept him through sickness and health. So I'll just have to be unhappy."

If you think assertive behavior is selfish, let me illustrate the meaning of two terms for you. *(a) Selfishness* is evident when a person wants something but does not feel obligated to repay the other party for making a sacrifice. Such people believe it is perfectly fine to receive benefits but not to give them. *(b) Self-interest* is evident when a person is concerned about his or her own welfare but doesn't expect to be treated nicely without having to pay for it. Self-interested people reciprocate and expect a fair exchange of services. They receive, but they are perfectly willing to give.

A woman who worked eight hours a day asked her husband to help with the dishes. He protested that this was woman's work and refused outright to cooperate. She asked me whether she was being selfish and I insisted she was being very self-interested instead. I suggested that she tell him that if he did not want to clean the dishes, she would not cook. As a result they ate out numerous times, and she often purchased the more expensive items on the menu. After several lobster dinners he began to feel a pinch on his wallet, and he agreed to help her out after supper. This made her much easier to get along with, and eventually they were both more happy than they would have been if she had allowed his uncooperativeness to continue.

There is no reason, however, for you to become any nastier than the situation warrants or more difficult than you need to be in order to get the results you want. Start off easily and mildly. If this does not work, increase your resistance until you do get results.

How successful can such tactics be? I have already admitted that they certainly do not always work, but I must add that it surprised me and my clients how frequently they do. If you have a reasonable cause for complaint and you assert yourself without bitterness—just firmness—and if you stick with your cold war long enough, you may very well be surprised at how nicely things will change. People are really quite loath to break up a marriage. It generally takes an enormous dissatisfaction over a long period of time to bring a marriage relationship to the point of total noncooperation. Before such a state is reached, most people will give in.

If you have certain religious prohibitions against separation and divorce, you will obviously have to tolerate more frustrations than those who don't have such prohibitions. You will have to learn to be less resentful but more resigned; you will have to hope that your good actions will eventually win your partner over by making him or her feel sorry for the bad treatment you are receiving.

THE MORAL ISSUE

I fully understand your reluctance to return harsh behavior for harsh behavior. As sensitive and caring people, we generally feel that it is ethically wrong to return one wrong for another. The old proverb that two wrongs don't make a right has a very convincing ring to it; and when I recommend that you kick others if they kick you, it would certainly seem as though I am urging you to commit a wrong as bad as the wrong that was done to you.

Such is not the case. When you do things to make others uncomfortable because you want to change their behavior for the better, you have to realize that they are the ones who have indirectly urged you to use the harsher method. I hope that all along you were more than willing to use more gentle methods and that you are now resorting to more extreme methods only because the gentler approach did not work. You have reasoned, shown patience, turned the other cheek, and tried to be a very decent person about the whole matter, but this didn't work. Should you continue on that passive and tolerant course indefinitely? To do so would only encourage more misbehavior.

Is it moral to fight evil, even if you have to use pain to do it? We assume that you are interested in changing someone else's unacceptable behavior. To do so you must extinguish that behavior by not rewarding it. That is the critical principle on which this whole argument rests. If you are eternally nice to someone who is mistreating you, then you are rewarding that person for being unkind. The only people who respond positively to your kind treatment are the unusually mature and stable ones; they can be shown with some patience that they are being unreasonable. The rest of humankind simply becomes programmed to become meaner and meaner.

To extinguish unacceptable behavior, however, it is up to you to do something; you have to penalize it. You will want to make the offending person so increasingly uncomfortable by your actions that he or she stops. That is the fair thing to do. This is the opposite of rewarding your partner for being selfish. It is punishing him or her for being rude. It is therefore perfectly true to state that you are being tough with others to help them even though they can't appreciate what you are doing. They may feel that you are being very unfair, inconsiderate, and quite mean. But if your resistance is meant to get the person to give up a bad habit, then ultimately you may be helping that individual.

If you refuse to pick up the family's dirty clothing because they won't put it in a hamper, and if they thereby learn to be cooperative and put the dirty wash where it belongs, have you hurt them or helped them? If you leave your girl friend at a party because she did not accept your warnings that you did not want her to flirt and drink too much, have you hurt her or helped her? To my mind, tough action with an offensive person is no different from taking 'a boy for a polio shot. Though the child may scream loud enough to be heard for three blocks, he still gets the shot because his mother and father know very well what a very loving act it is to protect the boy against polio. We sometimes help those we love by giving them *necessary* pain. And if we help people whom we love break bad habits that might eventually destroy our relationship with them, and if this causes them some temporary discomfort, then that's still the way it has to be. We are interested in the *long*-range effects our negative behavior may have. It becomes apparent, then, that it is well worth the effort to teach the family to be more responsible at home, to teach the girl friend to conduct herself more properly if she wants your company, and to teach the boy that a lifetime free from the threat of polio is worth a moment of pain. All these are efforts to teach loving acts.

If you look at the issue in this manner, I think you cannot fail to agree that being lenient and passive with people who are already behaving badly is an *immoral* act because it fosters more immoral behavior on their part. I further contend that you are not being immoral even when you behave as your opponent does, because his or her act was prompted either by ignorance or disturbance, while yours is prompted by a desire to teach that person not to continue such actions. The act may very well be the same, but your *intention* is on a much higher plane.

It is high time that people began to feel comfortable with their assertiveness. And if assertiveness does not work, then it is high time that they became comfortable with their aggressiveness. The difference between these two approaches is that assertiveness is trying to get your way without force or violence; aggression is getting your way with force and violence.

You may protest that surely there must be a better way to deal with the human condition than to resort to increasingly negative behavior until even violence is considered a moral position. I am afraid there is not. This reminds me of the protests that my couples in marriage counseling present to me when they, too, say that they wish they could do something other than what I am suggesting to them. Let me go over once more the choices we all have in facing unacceptable behavior. And let me show you the dilemmas caused by all of these choices.

I first point out that one can usually tolerate a bad situation with grace. If you can't do anything about a bad situation, learn to resign yourself to it. My clients often say they have reached a point where they cannot tolerate someone anymore. So I offer them the next option: Protest. They insist that this is something that bothers them too much and they do not want to sink to the other person's level. I suggest that they therefore leave the sit uation by a divorce or separation. "Oh, but that's too upsetting, and besides, my religion doesn't allow it." I then offer the fourth option, which is to tolerate the situation with resentment, but to expect the usual emotional problems that follow. They naturally have no taste for this, so I then say very seriously, "Well, then, why don't you tolerate it without resentment?" Then they point out that this is unacceptable, and around and around we go until they realize that all four choices are rather distasteful *and there are no others available.* A distasteful choice has to be made. Usually, the one they have the most hope for is trying to change the other person's behavior through protest (Option No. 2). This approach is also one of the stormiest. But if successful, it creates a condition that one might actually be able to live with. People sometimes learn best when they are hurt most.

MORAL RETARDATION

Consider this passage from the Good News Bible. It comes from the apostle Paul's first letter to the Corinthians, chapter 13, verses 4–7: "Love is patient and kind; it is not jealous or conceited or proud; love is not ill-mannered or selfish or irritable; love does not keep a record of wrongs; love is not happy with evil, but is happy with the truth. Love never gives up; and its faith, hope, and patience never fail."

Were more elegant words ever written? Can you imagine what this world would be like if people lived up to this teaching? It has beauty, majesty, and hope; and we would like it to apply to all situations. Reasonable people, stable persons, and those who are not terribly troubled can accept this statement of love as a way of life. Those who are seriously troubled or seriously immature, however, do not always respond to Paul's ideals. This way of love also does not seem to work with another class of persons whom I call "moral retardates."

Moral retardates are those who simply have a level of moral understanding that is far below what we would expect them to have in view of their age and experience. Just as one can give a score to people's intellectual performance, one can also approximate people's moral performance. Some individuals such as philanthropists might get a high score in moral behavior. Petty individuals, torturers, hateful and nasty people, or those who mean well but who create needless pain for others would get low moral scores.

A moral retardate is somebody who is not necessarily disturbed or intellectually retarded. Such a person is often quite intelligent, educated, and otherwise under at least

average emotional control. Yet his or her moral development could be so deficient that it ranks at the retarded
level when compared to the moral development of wise
and compassionate people. It is the moral retardates that
cannot be dealt with by Rule No. 2. They require the
painful consequences of Rule No. 3 to make them change.

There are numerous examples of moral retardation that
can be used to illustrate my point, but the most powerful
I can think of is the prejudice that has historically been
shown to blacks and to women. Blacks and females have
both been treated unjustly by perfectly decent people in
a white, male-dominated society. Those who approved
slavery and perpetuated discrimination, and the many
males in our society who still think women should not have
equal opportunities—these persons were and are normal,
stable, and in many ways healthy, moral people. Yet they
have committed injustices against millions. They are com-
mitting social injustices by violating the civil rights of half
the population. But if they are so healthy and moral, why
are they doing these things? Because in this area they are
simply moral retardates. They do not see the immorality
of their behavior. They have not been trained to put themselves into the place of others and to identify with their
suffering lives.

No matter how much you talk to moral retardates, it is
almost impossible to get them to see the rightness of your
cause. They think that because so many agree with them
they must be right. These people can come from the cen-
ter of the academic, legal, or religious worlds, yet they can
be the perpetrators of the greatest evils the world has ever
known. We need not go into the shabby history of slavery
in the United States or in other parts of the globe to docu-
ment this. I only ask you to realize that these practices
were sanctioned by people in the finest universities, by
persons from all political fields and all religions. Slavery
was preached as a proper human institution from many

pulpits. These were not wicked people, they were not emotionally disturbed, they were not neurotic. They simply lacked an understanding of moral behavior that extended beyond their immediate time and history.

Women have been abused, subjugated, and forced into second-class citizenship for thousands of years. And those perpetrating these injustices were and are frequently also respected, intelligent, and sophisticated, coming from some of the highest and most respected societies in the land. And they were and are moral retardates too, and that is why reasoning, being patient, and turning the other cheek simply do not work with such persons. Interestingly enough, in his second letter to the Corinthians (chapter 11, verses 19–20), the apostle Paul reprimands them because they "suffer fools gladly," tolerating and allowing themselves to be taken advantage of by domineering and insolent people. I suggest that we should not suffer moral retardates gladly either. Loving them endlessly and being unfailingly patient, as Paul earlier suggested, never seems to change such people. We do not have to hate them for their mistakes, but we had certainly better learn to resist their stupidity, their blindness, and their moral retardation.

Fortunately we can alter this sad human condition and teach people to be morally superior rather than retarded. And one of the ways to do it is to *return annoying behavior for annoying behavior.* This approach has actually been in use for centuries, and millions of people already practice it. But they do not understand that it has a very powerful moral base.

Consider the case of a woman who was abused by her alcoholic father for years, to the point where she simply lost all feeling for him. She has forgiven him for his mistreatment but now wants nothing to do with him. Is she morally correct in her rejection? I believe she is. He earned her rejection. She does not have to be angry with him, nor hate him. He is not an unworthy person. He is simply a human being who had problems that no one was able to stop at the time. If she finds no pleasure in his company, it is his fault. The fact that she does not hate the man does not mean she has to enjoy him or be of service to him.

When parents are so disgusted with their children that they cut them out of their wills, is this a moral act? Yes it is. To leave a fortune to a "brat" rewards the child for "brattiness." When parents leave an estate to others more deserving they teach their children the lesson that one has to earn the love and respect of others. Two sisters who had several conversations daily with each other developed a breach after the older girl threatened not to talk to her sister again if the youngest sister would not stop talking with a particular boy. The younger girl defied her sister, talked to her boyfriend, and has not had another word of conversation with her oldest sister in months. Did the younger sister act morally? Of course she did. To have acted otherwise would have placed the older girl in the position of a dictator over the younger one and effectively squelched her growth.

Compare the above examples of self-respect with the situation of a woman who told me that her husband treated her badly, emotionally and physically. She refused to punish him with even the slightest penalty for his abuse, saying, "He can't help it; he was an abused child." As noble as she may at first appear to be, she is actually fostering more abusive behavior by refusing to stop it. She is behaving neurotically. Long-suffering individuals who tolerate from their mates all manner of behavior, including drunkenness, beatings, infidelities, and nagging, are usually not displaying profound acts of forgiveness. All too often they are simply self-loathing people who do not believe they deserve better treatment and who therefore tolerate the most incredible unfairness from those closest to them.

A man once told me that his father forbade him ever to defend himself against children who might pick on him at school. He was a husky fellow and could easily have protected himself at any time, but he obeyed his father faithfully. The elderly gentleman went on the assumption that *(a)* punitive behavior was wrong, no matter what the provocation, and *(b)* eventually people would change. As a result, my subject was picked on and teased, shoved and hit by his schoolmates from the first grade to the twelfth. One day in his senior year he was thoroughly fed up with this injustice. He proceeded to beat up one of the worst offenders and shoved him into a hall locker. Was he right to do this? He should have been given a medal. How many more years did his father think he had to wait before he saw moral behavior develop in the other children? President Theodore Roosevelt was certainly not far from the mark when he expressed Rule No. 3 in his own words: "Speak softly and carry a big stick."

Obstacles to Using Rule No. 3

Some people have such dissatisfying arrangements at work or in their marriages that separation of some kind is about the only sensible solution they can find. Yet people who are in the most ridiculous kinds of marriages will also tell themselves that they "don't believe in divorce."

I once knew a man who was insanely jealous of his wife and made her live according to his rules and expectations to such a degree that she was an extremely unhappy woman. He successfully convinced her that divorce was immoral and totally unacceptable, and she was browbeaten enough to accept his arguments. She therefore made it possible for him to do whatever he wanted in his marriage. He could be impossible and inconsiderate and know that he would never lose his wife, because she was convinced that even a separation was unthinkable. How is anything to change if she doesn't have the ultimate weapon? Why should he change? He had carte blanche to abuse and dominate his wife without being the slightest bit affected by any pressure she might be able to exert against him.

But some people will not use Rule No. 3 and put pressures on their partners, because they are afraid a divorce will demonstrate that they have failed. Even though they may have been married for thirty-five years, they still think that a broken marriage is a failure. You have never failed in marriage as long as you have tried. If you have made marriage work for one week or fifty years, you can always say you made it succeed for that period of time. If you couldn't or didn't want to carry it any farther than that simply because you knew it wouldn't work, you'd be sensible to leave. Perhaps your partner didn't understand your desires and needs and was making no effort to keep you interested in the marriage. Then it would make sense for you to break a relationship that could no longer be a satisfying one. If you can do better by leaving a sinking ship, leave it. When we begin to see that marriage is like a job we quit when we can't stand it, we will stop being ashamed of getting a separation. I am not suggesting, of course, that we get rid of our mates as readily as we quit jobs. But I do insist that when things get bad enough and you are becoming disturbed, falling out of love is the best solution for you. As I have said before, people do not make such decisions quickly or without considerable suffering. They may quit jobs on the spur of the moment, but most people anguish about leaving a marriage.

It is about time we were taught to think with our heads and not with our hearts. I am sure there are times when we do not want to be superrational; we want our feelings to dictate our actions. No sensible person would offer the argument that it is better to think like a computer in every instance. Life simply wouldn't be much fun, because it wouldn't have much color or excitement.

It is also about time, however, that we stopped putting down the amazing abilities of the brain as a tool by which we can solve our problems. Why shouldn't we think with our heads when we are talking about selecting a mate? Why shouldn't we think with our heads when we want to decide if we are going to have one child or ten? We think carefully when we buy clothes, cars, and homes, although our feelings certainly enter into these decisions. If you buy a car on the basis of feelings alone, however, and discover later that the thing guzzles gasoline at such an alarming rate that it threatens to make a pauper out of you, you will wish you had used your head instead of your heart.

Do you want to know where the seat of power is in any relationship? Isn't it with the person who cares the least? If a relationship is too important to you, you are likely to give in too much to preserve it and you will buy it at too great a price. If you are not excessively attached to something, however, you can deal with losing it much more easily; and you can drive a harder bargain. In a marriage this means that the one who cares for it the least is going to get his or her way more often. The less caring person can always say, "If you don't like it, you can leave." That's the way you would talk if your job were not terribly important to you. But if your very life depended on your job and the family were going to be put out on the street if you didn't have it, then you probably wouldn't rock the boat at any time, for fear of the boss's disapproval. I find this highly unfair, but life is like that.

A middle-aged man was in the habit of spending several nights a week playing cards with his buddies at the local tavern. He put on weight from the food and beer, and this gave him a waistline that his wife found most unattractive. That, plus the fact that he would leave her at home feeling rejected and lonely, brought her to my office for consultation. She was concerned both about her feelings for her husband and the state of their marriage. I learned that the marriage was essentially a sound one and that her husband was basically a very decent fellow except for the behavior that was distressing her. I advised her to tell him what her complaints were. Specifically, she wanted him to lose weight so that she could be more attracted to him sexually; and she wanted him to control his drinking so that he did not come home reeking of alcohol. She also wanted him to socialize more with her and not so much with his male companions.

She went home and talked with him about her complaints and reported back to me in a week what his reaction was. It turned out (much to my surprise) that he was absolutely adamant in his unwillingness to change. At this point I called in the husband in the hope that I might be able to get him to see what was happening to his marriage and that a few adjustments on his part would not bother him much but would make a considerable difference to his wife. We had a very pleasant conversation, but he was as firm with me as he was with her. He believed he was in the right and could not see that she had a legitimate cause for complaint. I suggested that the issue was actually so important to his wife that she might begin to protest in some form or other to register her point more strongly. He was unfazed by this and simply reassured me that if she had to do that, she had to do it.

I next saw the wife and told her that we had presented our case quite clearly, but still her husband disagreed. I felt he had thought through his viewpoint very thoroughly and simply could not accept our reasoning. Therefore it was up to her not to become upset over his refusal and not to continue flogging a dead horse by pressing him over and over to see her viewpoint. Instead, I advised her to make him so uncomfortable with his life-style that he would be willing to change.

Soon she began neglecting the laundry and the housekeeping and even began to withdraw sexually. He refused to budge. By now it was beginning to appear to her that he was unshakable in his resolve and that he would stick to his guns even if he had to go to the divorce court. That she did not want. Thus, when she became convinced that he was not going to change no matter what kind of pressures she put on him, she dropped her tactics and gave in. She reasoned that being alone several nights a week and having a husband who was developing a sloppy figure was more tolerable than getting upset or taking the consequences of a divorce.

We cannot know for certain what would have happened had she persisted in her strategy and not given in. But in this case evidently the husband felt his principles were more important than his marriage, and it did indeed appear as though he would rather lose the latter than the former. This is where he got his strength, and it is why he evidently won out in this contest.

This brings up an interesting point in connection with communication. At no time in this relationship could it ever be said that these people were not communicating. For years now I have been aware of the tendency to interpret most difficulties between parties as a result of poor communication. I have never agreed with that theory, and the above example illustrates my point. This man and this woman were telling each other exactly what they felt. Each knew the other's reasons for his or her behavior in all the detail that was necessary. Still they did not agree. Was it because they did not understand each other? Of course not. Each understood the other completely but simply did not accept the other person's reasoning. This happens all the time between people and between governments. What we have to recognize is that sometimes we must *agree to disagree.* It is naive to suppose that if we explain ourselves fifteen more times, our listener will then understand us and agree with us.

George had spent his adult life being a decent human being. He worked at it consciously because he believed that sainthood was possible and could be achieved with great effort and resolute design. And he valued saintliness above all. To no one's surprise he became a minister, and in this profession he could pursue his ideals steadfastly. His charm, intelligence, and basic decency gained him respect and love from a wide circle, both inside and outside the congregation. His church was full, his popularity at its peak, and his good works unquestioned. So why did he need to see me?

Because he was falling out of love. The loss of feeling for his wife was growing, and he had not been able to reverse it. At times thoughts of divorce were so strong that they shocked him. It troubled him deeply to realize that at times he could very easily turn his back on June, his wife of about fifteen years. Guilt over these reflections came naturally to his finely tuned sense of morality. He had promised to love her "till death us do part." But for two years he had struggled to push back the nagging truth that he wanted out.

He was fully aware of the impact this would have on his career. If it would not harm him greatly, it certainly would not help. His four children were at ages when divorce would be especially troubling to them. Above and beyond these problems was his belief that to move toward divorce would simply be in bad taste and poor form; and it was ethically unacceptable.

George wanted to change his wife, or himself, or both. It wasn't that he hadn't tried; that's not why he felt so exasperated. It was his lack of success. June's annoying habits surfaced slowly over the years. At first, shortly after George was ordained, she was still the lighthearted and fun-loving girl he had courted. With every move up to a bigger church and a more prestigious congregation, however, June lost more of the joy of living and became more and more rigid. To cover her lifelong insecurities she paid homage to the god of perfection. Anything less than the best in her children, husband, self, or home was unacceptable and viewed as a threat to her self-esteem. The inevitable consequence was clearly that she would become difficult to love and live with.

In our first session, George reviewed how he had coped with this problem: "I tried to ignore her demands at first. Sometimes that worked rather nicely. Just as often, however, I'd find myself so annoyed at June's fussiness that I just couldn't hold back. Then we'd quarrel. I'd lose my cool and say things to hurt her. Then I'd feel guilty all day. I don't like being that way. It goes against everything I stand for."

He went on to point out that he and the children had been "walking on eggshells" to avoid her getting critical. Most of the time this maintained the peace. Every so often there would be minor explosions against her "tyranny," but in a day or two tempers always cooled and the family would be stepping to her tune once more.

As nearly as I could determine, George resorted to verbal protests in reasoning with June. If he made himself clear once, he made himself clear a thousand times. June knew precisely what he thought about kids coming home late or getting average grades. He communicated his views on how it was perfectly fine to joke with the parishioners and their wives. She disagreed. To her, he lost their respect when he allowed them to treat him as an equal and when he let everyone address him by his first name. This was a family that communicated quite well. That was seldom the problem. It was the lack of agreement which caused so much tension.

It seemed abundantly clear to me that he had relied too long on the gentle and persuasive methods of Rule No. 2

to change his wife. He repeated himself endlessly, trying to get his wife to understand an issue from his viewpoint, as though she did not comprehend what he was saying.

Therapist: Why can't you see that she simply disagrees? Surely you can't think another year or two of giving her your reasons why you want her to change is going to succeed, do you?

George: I'm almost sure you're right. God knows I've made my views known from every conceivable point. I just don't know how to convince her.

T: Why don't you stop being such a nice guy and give up your logical arguments for a few powerful acts?

George: Like what? You're not suggesting I get physical are you?

T: Certainly not, at least in the way you're thinking. But it is time for you to *do* something instead of *say* something.

George: Do what?

T: Any number of things. I'm not familiar enough with you or your wife to know what levers you can push.

George: Levers I can lower on her? I don't want to lower the boom on my wife. I want her to relax, stop being so blasted self-conscious and fussy with all of us, and just enjoy life more.

T: I can't disagree with you. What you say makes a lot of sense. However, after years of trying to talk her into behaving as you prefer, what results have you gotten?

George: Not much.

T: Then isn't it about time you changed your strategy and stopped reinforcing her behavior? Perhaps if you would stop being . . .

George: Excuse me for interrupting, Doctor, but what do you mean, "stop reinforcing her behavior"? Who's reinforcing her behavior? I've fought it for years until I'm blue in the face.

T: You're rewarding her and thus reinforcing her ways. Why do you think she still acts this way after years of scolding her?

George: It certainly isn't because I condone it. You admit I've been giving her a bad time scolding her. So how can you think she's being encouraged?

T: If the behavior exists, George, it exists because it's being rewarded. Behavior that is not rewarded or reinforced is eventually extinguished.

George: But how can that be? I've never praised her for being constantly moody. I've never kissed her for yelling at the kids. And I've never hugged her for criticizing me for being friendly with members of my congregation.

T: I don't doubt that. Still, I insist, if people are behaving in a particular way toward you it's because you allow them to do so. If you didn't tolerate her annoying ways, either she would change, or you would resign yourself to them without resentment, or you would separate or divorce. Since she's doing the same annoying things to the family, I must conclude she's getting strokes from you for being annoying.

George: How? How can I possibly be giving her rewards while I'm doing nothing but protesting? I don't understand.

T: I think you just gave the answer. You were doing nothing but talk. Talk is cheap. Most people can let talk go in one ear and out the other. I suggest June was probably uncomfortable during those times *but* not uncomfortable enough to change.

George: Even when I stormed out of the house at times, or when she left the room in tears?

T: Answer the question yourself.

George: Why do you ask me to do that?

T: Because the answer is obvious.

George: You mean, I suppose, that if nothing happened when I left, or when she cried, then she was still getting more pleasure somehow than the pain I gave her.

T: Precisely.

George: But where and how was the pleasure coming from?

T: Probably from her getting her way again. I suspect you yelled a lot but ended up giving in to her practically all the time.

George: But I had to. If I gave her too much opposition, she'd reject me for days on end. There wouldn't be any affection and her anger at me would overflow onto the kids.

T: I'm sure that isn't pleasant, and I can understand why you'd want to avoid frustrating her.

George: You can say that again.

T: However, my point still stands. Whenever you ignore unacceptable behavior, for whatever reason, it's likely to remain unchanged or get worse.

George: I've got to think this through. I know what you say makes sense, but it's hard to swallow.

I was attempting in this session and in subsequent visits to motivate him to give up being verbal and tolerant. Already he was a perfect example of dozens of people whom I have counseled who were no longer *just reasonably content.*

T: George, I don't want you to avoid doing something about June, because if you let her have her way at the cost of making yourself less than reasonably content, you will actually be hurting yourself and the kids, as well as your wife.

George: I don't get it. How in heaven's name am I going to harm the whole family by giving June her way?

T: By bringing yourself below your JRC. That's the point where you're just reasonably content. Fall below that point and everyone is in trouble.

George: You mean that? If I'm badly frustrated, the whole family's in trouble?

T: I'm not talking about normal frustrations. I'm talking about chronic frustrations, the ones that go on for months and years. When you feel you're not even barely satisfied in a relationship—any kind of relationship—three bad things happen, George.

George: What are they?

T: First, you become upset, troubled, depressed. You bite your nails, or have nightmares, or drink, or have thoughts of infidelity.

George: I haven't had thoughts of cheating, thank God, but some of those other symptoms are definitely there. What are the other two points?

T: The second consequence of being chronically frustrated with a loved one is that you gradually but surely fall out of love. The third consequence is that you lose interest in the marriage itself.

George: I see. It seems that I've felt all three, wouldn't you say?

T: That's the way I see it, yes. To prevent things from getting worse, you had better do something about reversing these results.

George: I see, or else you think I'll lose more feeling for June and eventually the marriage might end.

T: Right. If you ignore your own deepest desires and

needs, June will feel great at first, but you'll get more miserable. Then she'll suffer too. I suggest you make her less content and make yourself more content.

George: What if she protests?

T: What if she does? In fact, you can depend on her doing just that. However, your question is irrelevant. It makes no difference whether she's unhappy or not. The only thing I want you to focus on for the present is whether or not you're at the JRC.

George: Isn't it possible that I'll send June into a condition of low contentment if I pressure her to please me more?

T: Certainly.

George: Then what?

T: Then both of you can try using Option No. 1 and tolerate the frustrations without resentment. For example, you could talk yourself into not minding her nagging. Or she could do the same about your complaints.

George: I'm not sure we aren't past that point.

T: I suspect you are. So, as I see it, you're best off if you go on strike or declare a cold war until you get the kind of behavior from June that will make you love her again.

He was beginning to see the strategy. In principle it met with his approval. In practice it bothered him considerably. Getting nasty with his wife went against his gentle nature.

George: I can't tell you how offensive I find your suggestion that I give June a bad time. The very thought of lowering myself to her immaturities bothers me. Her demandingness is bad enough without my acting just like her.

T: I sympathize with you completely. Look at it this way. If giving her a taste of her own medicine and making her uncomfortable when she becomes very unpleasant stops that behavior, then what have you lost but a little pride? Remember, you tried for years talking to her with logic, reason, and patience, and the result of trying to reach her on your higher level is that she's worse than ever, while you're more unhappy than ever.

George: Yes, that's right. You said it.

T: So what do you have to lose if you communicate at her level? Speak her language and you may just get through for the first time.

George: I seriously doubt that this is going to work.

T: Why do you say that?

George: Because these tactics are going to raise such a stink that we're going to get into worse fights. The only thing that has helped this marriage is my backing down when she became demanding and loud. If I had not given in, she would have become furious and I would have gotten so angry I'd have said lots of things I didn't mean.

T: Oh, I see why you're hesitating. You're thinking your getting angry over her anger is like throwing gasoline on her fire.

George: It sure is.

T: But I wouldn't for one moment want you to be angry while you're trying to make her uncomfortable.

We then went into the RET theory of anger in great detail. I pointed out to him that he is the only person who makes himself angry. He does this by thinking (a) that he has to have his way, (b) that people who frustrate him are bad, and (c) that to change a bad person into a good person one has to be very punishing and hateful.

Between us we decided that ignoring her outbursts was the first step. We figured that she would get more upset for a time and put the marriage under its greatest strain ever. However, I reasoned that if he held out and politely stayed out of her way and did his thing despite her protests, she would see he was serious.

In the following weeks I coached him on how to frustrate her in the hope of breaking her bad habits, and on how to do this calmly. For example, if she criticized him at a social function, he was to take her home then and there, after politely bidding the host and hostess good night.

If she made any purchase that cost more than the price on which they had agreed, he was to call up the store and have the item returned. If a check was already written for the item, he was to notify the bank immediately and stop payment. If she refused to spend a fair number of weekends and holidays with his parents, he was to refuse to visit hers.

She had a habit of keeping him waiting. When he felt the time of delay had reached the point of thoughtlessness, he was to tell her nicely that he was going and that she could use her car to get herself to their appointment. He was not to argue with her, just give her a peck on the cheek, smile, and say, "See you there soon, honey." And then he was to leave without her.

George: That was one of the hardest things to do that you can imagine. I hated being so petty. Me, a minister, acting like a spoiled brat. Yet, since I've been paying her back in kind I want you to know things are definitely changing. I sense it every week. You told me she had no respect for me. Well, I'm slowly getting it now, and I'm very pleased. If I had known this years ago, I'd never have let things go on so long.

T: Do you understand why you were so passive?

George: I've thought about that, Dr. Hauck, and I think

there are really two reasons. The first is that I didn't want to rock the boat and have my marriage in trouble. After all, I am a minister and I'm in the business of counseling people. Well, you can imagine how it would look if I had a bad marriage or, worse yet, if I got a divorce.

T: What was your second reason?

George: The second is more a matter of principle. I have always been taught that love can conquer all. If people are not happy with each other, we are supposed to love them and accept them until they become more loving. From what I've learned in therapy I can now see that unconditional love can lead to emotional crippling, while being firm with our loved ones can be a very strong expression of love. We do that with our children; why shouldn't it work on an adult-to-adult level?

T: I couldn't have said that any better.

June eventually felt bothered enough that she wanted some control over all the "crazy" things that were coming out of therapy. So she called to see me. I gave her about six sessions alone, and then we had a few more with George.

The results were most gratifying. George became less tolerant of June's unacceptable behavior because he wasn't so worried about her leaving. This gave June a better feeling about him, since she liked his strong hand. Incidentally, both seemed slightly surprised by this discovery. The relationship improved steadily. In fact, some of the lessons George learned from Rational-Emotive Therapy and my views on assertiveness were later used in dealing with his children and even his church staff.

The most satisfying evidence of his change appeared in a couple of sermons incorporating his new views on cooperation, respect, and love.

George: It wasn't easy to advise my people to show love through firmness, because I knew they would regard that as revenge and reject it.

T: I can understand that easily enough. It takes a lot of rethinking of old ideas to realize that giving people all they want can cause them not to respect or love us.

George: And that not being nice to a fault is the better way to love and be loved. However, I am still reluctant to act that way. Will I ever change?

T: It may get easier, but I think most people of goodwill are always going to feel reluctant when they are pushed to get tough. And I'm glad that's so. When we enjoy getting mean, we're in trouble.

George: Amen.

A REALISTIC POINT OF VIEW

Much to my sorrow, I have come to the conclusion that because of the nature of humankind, serious conflicts among us are inevitable. Violence and murder—even war —are inevitable. It appears that the only way these drastic outcomes can be avoided is if Rules No. 1 and No. 2 always work. That seems to me to be a farfetched hope. It is highly unlikely that people and nations will always be so gracious as to reciprocate good deeds or to be patient and understanding when complaint is made against them. It is far more likely that in any dispute we will often not be able to see the correctness of the other person's position and will defend our own viewpoint to the death.

It is ironic that a method that has such therapeutic value should also have such fatal consequences if overused. As I have tried to demonstrate, it is perfectly correct and scientifically sound to use penalties and punishments in order to rid people of objectionable behaviors. There is a delicate balance, however, between making people so uncomfortable that they will change and making them so uncomfortable that they want to kill. No doubt the terrorists of the world would all claim that they have been pushed to the wall by a society that was deaf to their pleas. They would undoubtedly insist that their extreme tactics were necessary, since all other methods failed. And believing that milder methods will be totally ineffective, they have felt pushed to use inhuman ones. And so we have kidnappings with demands for huge sums of money, the spraying of airports with machine-gun fire, the bombing of innocent civilian groups by remote control, or the shooting of kneecaps off public officials.

Is violence ever justified? Can violent acts be moral? Only if we could prove that violent measures are the only ones that work against an evil could we argue that evil means bring good ends. Our only hope for a sane world is that those who are in power have some sense of morality. If healthy persons prevail, then Rule No. 3 will be used sparingly and cautiously. If neurotic people are in power, we will have terror, war, and hell. Rule No. 3 is not at fault; the way it is used is at fault. That is why I advocate the application of Rule No. 3 only as a last resort. This rule, along with the penetrating lessons from the psychology of the Rational-Emotive school, *can* contribute to loving relationships when employed lovingly.

Conclusion: You Can Do It

    I wrote this book because I felt compelled to do so. I have been dealing with people who have struggled with intimate relationships and were extremely unhappy over them. Some of the greatest suffering I have encountered on a daily basis has been that of people who have not been happy at work, with their families, or in their marriages. I have tried to understand the causes of this discontent and have come to formulate my reciprocity theory of love and my business theory of marriage; and I have offered the three rules for achieving cooperation, respect, and love.

    I have seen the lives of individuals change when they have looked reality squarely in the face and have followed these three steps whenever necessary and as far as necessary. I know that you too can face frustrations, change the behavior of others, and bring a reasonable amount of happiness back into your life.

    Try always to remember that too much other-pity can hurt those you love. Take the attitude, "I love you enough to want to stop you from becoming the sort of person I can't tolerate."

    Remember that healthy love requires that you give to another all he or she *needs,* not all he or she wants. What we *need* is physical satisfaction and a roof over our heads. But there also are other kinds of needs—the need to be firm with others, the need to face challenges, the need to be tested by adversity, the need to take risks, and the need to face life with our own resources. Giving is unquestionably a loving act. Not giving—with the absence of a vengeful heart—can be the greatest love act of all.

Overcome your fear of showing appreciation and tenderness by returning kindness with kindness. That is the first face of love.

Overcome your anger at faults and be forgiving. That is the second face of love.

Overcome guilt and other-pity so you can be firm and intolerant of meanness. That is the third face of love.

Recommended Readings

Ellis, Albert. *How to Live with a Neurotic.* Rev. ed., Crown Publishers, 1975.

———, and Harper, Robert A. *A New Guide to Rational Living.* Prentice-Hall, 1975.

Hauck, Paul. *The Rational Management of Children.* 2d rev. ed., Libra Publishers, 1972.

———. *Overcoming Depression.* Westminster Press, 1973.

———. *Overcoming Frustration and Anger.* Westminster Press, 1974.

———. *Overcoming Worry and Fear.* Westminster Press, 1975.

———. *How to Do What You Want to Do: The Art of Self-Discipline.* Westminster Press, 1976.

———. *Marriage Is a Loving Business.* Westminster Press, 1977.

———. *How to Stand Up for Yourself.* Westminster Press, 1979.

———. *Brief Counseling with RET* (Rational-Emotive Therapy). Westminster Press, 1980.

———. *Overcoming Jealousy and Possessiveness.* Westminster Press, 1981.

Krumboltz, John D., and Krumboltz, Helen B. *Changing Children's Behavior.* Prentice-Hall, 1972.

Madsen, Charles H., and Madsen, Clifford K. *Teaching/Discipline: A Positive Approach to Educational Development.* 3d ed., Allyn & Bacon, 1980.

Maslow, Abraham. *Motivation and Personality.* Harper & Brothers, 1954.

Maultsby, Maxie C., Jr. *Help Yourself to Happiness Through Rational Self-Counseling.* Institute for Rational Living, 1975.

Patterson, Gerald R. *Living with Children: New Methods for Parents and Teachers.* Rev. ed., Research Press, 1976.

Rachman, Stanley, and Teasdale, John. *Aversion Therapy and*

173

Behavior Disorders: An Analysis. University of Miami Press, 1969.

Skinner, B. F. *Beyond Freedom and Dignity.* Alfred A. Knopf, 1971.

Wolpe, Joseph, and Lazarus, Arnold A. *Behavior Therapy Techniques: A Guide to the Treatment of Neuroses.* Pergamon Press, 1968.